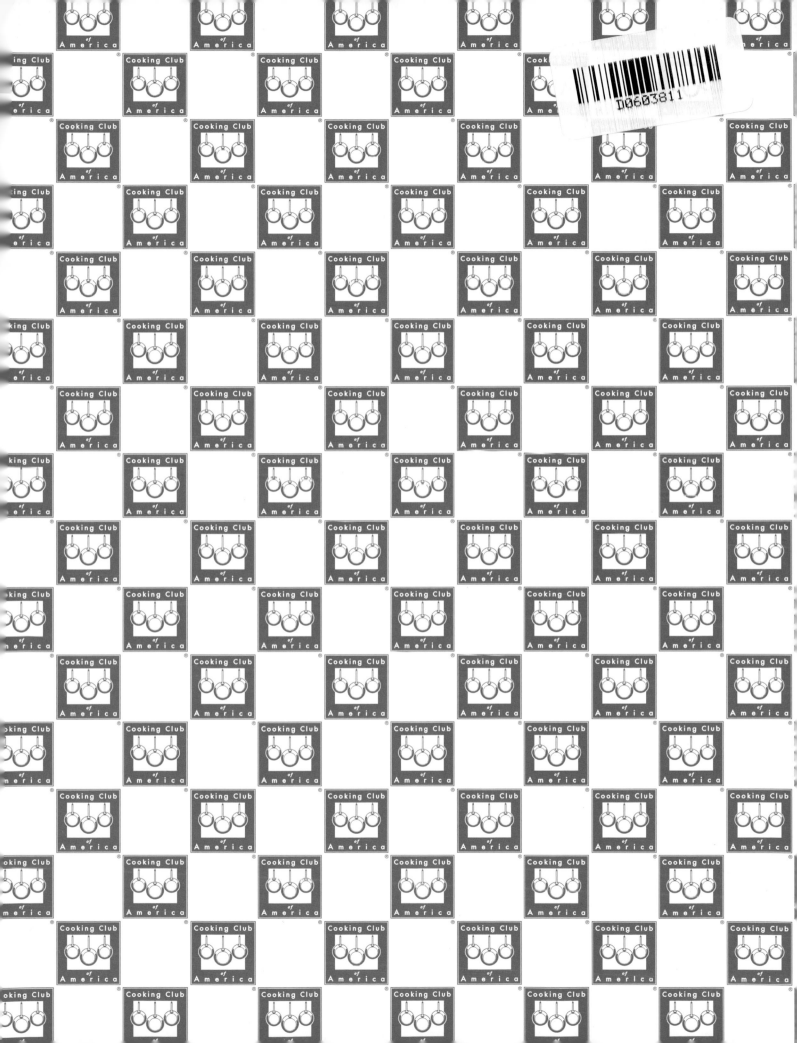

$\mathcal{T}$ODAY'S COUNTRY COOKING

Cooking Arts Collection™

CREDITS

About the Author  Minnesota native **Chef John Schumacher** has an extraordinary range of culinary experience, specializing in wild game and Central European cuisine. Internationally known, John has authored several cookbooks, including *Wild Game Cooking Made Easy*, *Fish Cooking Made Easy* and *John Schumacher's New Prague Hotel Cookbook*.

TODAY'S COUNTRY COOKING

Printed in 2006.

Tom Carpenter, Creative Director
Jennifer Guinea, Senior Book Development Coordinator
Tad Ware & Company, Inc.:   Book Design and Production
                                 Photography
                                 Food Styling
                                 Recipe Testing

On Cover: Scaloppini, page 106.
On Page 1: Cranberry Loaf, page 159.

6 7 8 / 08 07 06
©2001 Cooking Club of America
ISBN 1-58159-129-2

Cooking Club of America
12301 Whitewater Drive
Minnetonka, MN 55343
www.cookingclub.com

$\mathcal{T}$ABLE OF CONTENTS

*I*NTRODUCTION

"To cook is to love. To love is to cook." — Chef John

This book is dedicated to my mother, Helen, the best cook in our family. Thank you for teaching me that good enough is *never* good enough.

Today's Country Cooking is based on my 50-plus years of eating, cooking, and being cooked for by three generations of great farm and small-town homemakers, all descendents of Germany, Sweden and Norway. These hard-working mothers, wives and partners held family as their highest priority.

In my native rural Midwest, tradition is important, as it is throughout the world. Cooks prepare the best food available to them in the best way they know how, drawing from traditions (see me, love me, respect me through food) and new ideas. Meal times are for sharing stories of today and days past, as well as days to come.

We have very few truly new foods in this world of ours and, all in all, food is much the same as it was a century ago. Olives still have pits. Tomatoes (if home or small-farm grown) taste the same. Pork is still pork (albeit much leaner). Eggs still have yolks and whites. Fish have bones. Birds have gizzards. And so on.

But we do have a lot of new cooking techniques and trends. Some are good, and are incorporated into this book, alongside the tried-and-true traditions I grew up with and use to this day in my New Prague Hotel Restaurant. I will cook for you here the best I have, the best way I know, combining the old and the new into unique country tastes for today.

Chef August Ascof wrote his first classic, *The Esc of Piov Cookbook*, on the principles I'm talking about here — combining the technology of his time with tried-and-true recipes and formulas of the past. August Ascof wrote his book in the early 1900s. Here at the start of a new century, I strive to

bring the old and new together once again.

To me, cooking is love, sharing, hospitality, generosity and camaraderie all rolled into one. Along with my best recipes, I hope you find all that and more in *Today's Country Cooking*.

ＢASIC RECIPES

These recipes are the building blocks of good cuisine, whether the end product is "country" or not. It's important to have this solid foundation of recipes — and prepare each one well and consistently — because they affect the way many other dishes (in this book and beyond) turn out. You'll use this reference section of "building block" recipes often.

Farmers' Wives' Jam Made with Fresh Fruit or Berries, page 26

BEEF STOCK

This very important recipe will provide the base for many sauces and soups.

  5 lb. beef bones, cut into 4-inch pieces
2½ cups diced onions (1 inch)
2½ cups diced celery (1 inch)
1½ cups diced carrots (1 inch)
1½ gallons water
  2 cups crushed tomatoes
  1 recipe prepared *Sachet Bag* (page 14)

❶ Heat oven to 375°F.

❷ Rinse bones and pat dry. Place in roasting pan; bake one hour, turning occasionally, until browned.

❸ Add onions, celery and carrots to roasting pan; bake until vegetables are golden brown. Transfer browned bones, vegetables and drippings to Dutch oven. Add water; simmer over low heat 3 hours, skimming off fat and foam occasionally. Add tomatoes and Sachet Bag; simmer an additional 3 hours, skimming off fat and foam. Pour liquid through fine strainer; discard bones and vegetables.

❹ Return liquid to heat; bring to a fast boil, reducing by one-third. Cool; store in refrigerator up to 4 days.

4 quarts.

CHICKEN STOCK

After you remove the chicken meat from the bones, use it for sandwiches and salads.

3½ lb. chicken wings
  2 cups diced onions (1 inch)
1½ cups diced celery (1 inch)
1½ cups diced carrots (1 inch)
  4 quarts water
  1 recipe prepared *Sachet Bag* (page 14)

❶ Rinse chicken and pat dry.

❷ In large pot, combine chicken, onions, celery, carrots, water and Sachet Bag; simmer over low heat 3½ hours, skimming off excess fat and foam occasionally. Remove from heat; strain, reserving liquid.

❸ Return liquid to pot; bring to a fast boil. Cook until liquid is reduced by one-half. Skim off fat; strain. Cool; store in refrigerator up to 4 days.

4 quarts.

SEASONED FLOUR

Use white pepper so that the flour does not appear to have black flecks. Never reuse excess flour.

1   cup all-purpose flour
2   teaspoons salt
1/8   teaspoon white pepper

 In large bowl, combine flour, salt and pepper; mix well.
1 cup.

CLARIFIED BUTTER

This is sometimes known as "drawn butter."

1   lb. butter

 In medium saucepan, melt butter over low heat; skim off foam. Remove saucepan from heat; cool until all milk solids have fallen to bottom of pot. With ladle, remove all clear oil (clarified butter). Store in refrigerator.
3/4 cup.

WHIPPED CREAM

Whipped Cream *will stiffen upon refrigeration.*

1   cup heavy cream
1   tablespoon sugar
1/2   teaspoon vanilla

 Chill large bowl with ice; drain well. Place cream, powdered sugar and vanilla in bowl. Whip at medium speed until stiff. Transfer whipped cream to another large bowl; cover. Store in refrigerator.
8 (1/2 cup) servings.

EGG WASH

If you need only a small amount of egg wash, make one-half batch.

2   eggs
1/4   cup milk

 Break eggs into large bowl; add milk. Whisk mixture until frothy.
1/3 cup.

PIE CRUST *Pictured at right*

In a 9-inch pie plate, the bottom pie crust should weigh 8 oz; the top crust should weigh 7 oz. Everyone needs a good Pie Crust recipe — here's mine. Enjoy!

>   2   cups all-purpose flour
>   1   teaspoon salt
> 1¼   cups vegetable shortening
> ⅔   cup ice-cold water

❶ Heat oven to 350°F.

❷ In large bowl, combine flour, salt and shortening. Toss until mixture crumbles. Add water. Combine dough just enough to hold together. Roll out crust onto pastry cloth or flour-dusted cutting board.

❸ For pie shells, prick crust with fork. Place in 9-inch pie plate; gently shake to shrink dough. Place another 9-inch pie plate on top, sandwiching crust between pie plates; trim excess dough from edges. Bake 15 to 18 minutes or until light golden brown.

4 (8-oz.) crusts.

CHEF'S NOTES:

• Too much flour will make the crust tough.

• Always remember to shake crust after putting in pan, to shrink it.

• Leftover Pie Crust dough freezes well. Cut into proper weight and freeze in individual bags.

ROUX

Sauces and gravies are two of the most important components of great cooking. Roux thickens sauces and gravies. Although roux is only one of many cooking thickeners, I have concluded it is the best after 20 years of professional cooking.

>   1   lb. butter or margarine
>   1   lb. all-purpose flour

❶ Heat oven to 375°F.

❷ Heat butter in 2-quart casserole until melted; stir in flour. Bake one hour, stirring mixture every 15 minutes until golden brown and consistency of sand.

3 cups.

CHEF'S NOTES:

• You should weigh the flour for this recipe and not measure it.

• It is always better to use Roux at room temperature. The Roux keeps well in the refrigerator or freezer.

PAN GRAVY (BROWN SAUCE)

This is the best base for a great brown gravy.

6   tablespoons butter or margarine
1   cup diced onions (1/4 inch)
1/2 cup diced celery (1/4 inch)
1/2 cup diced carrots (1/4 inch)
2/3 cup all-purpose flour
6   cups prepared *Beef Stock* (page 8)
1/4 cup tomato puree
1   bay leaf
1   teaspoon salt
1/2 teaspoon freshly ground pepper

❶ In large pot, heat butter over medium heat until hot and bubbly; sauté onions, celery and carrots until onions are transparent. Stir in flour; reduce heat to low and cook an additional 2 minutes, stirring frequently with wooden spoon.

❷ In another large pot, heat stock to a boil, stirring slowly and constantly. Stir in flour mixture.

❸ Add tomato puree, bay leaf, salt and pepper; simmer 30 minutes. Add more salt and pepper, if desired. Strain and serve.

8 servings.

CHEF'S NOTES:

• If you don't have homemade Beef Stock, you can use canned broth.

• To make double strength Beef Stock, reduce 12 cups to 6 cups by rapidly boiling in a large saucepan.

• If you have any gravy left over, freeze it in 1 cup amounts in heavy-duty freezer bags. As you need more gravy, let bags thaw in refrigerator before heating and serving.

BASIC SALAD DRESSING SAUCE

Use this nice sauce for meat, potato or macaroni salads.

1   cup mayonnaise
2   teaspoons mustard
1   tablespoon sugar
1 1/2 teaspoons lemon juice
1/2 teaspoon salt
1/2 teaspoon white pepper
2   teaspoons Worcestershire sauce

❶ In large bowl, combine mayonnaise, mustard, sugar, lemon juice, salt, pepper and Worcestershire; mix until smooth. Keep covered 2 to 3 weeks in refrigerator.

1 1/4 cups.

THOUSAND ISLAND DRESSING

I use this homemade Thousand Island Dressing *in so much cooking.*

1	cup sour cream
2	cups mayonnaise
2	hard-cooked eggs, diced (1/4 inch)
3/4	cup chili sauce
1/4	cup ketchup
1	small red bell pepper, diced (1/4 inch)
1 1/2	tablespoons chopped fresh parsley (leaves only)
1	teaspoon lemon juice
1	teaspoon Worcestershire sauce
1/2	teaspoon freshly ground pepper
1	teaspoon salt

❶ In large bowl, combine sour cream, mayonnaise, eggs, chili sauce, ketchup, bell pepper, parsley, lemon juice, Worcestershire, pepper and salt; mix together gently but thoroughly.

❷ Store, covered, in refrigerator up to 30 days.

1 quart.

CHEF'S NOTES:

• To make Russian dressing, add 1/2 cup black caviar. Fold in gently.

• To make Sauce Remoulade, add 1 tablespoon capers and 10 anchovies, finely minced.

SACHET BAG

The purpose of a Sachet Bag is to produce a balance of seasoning for stocks and soups, while being able to remove all spice ingredients when desired. The reason for the bag is to be able to remove spices from the liquid. You could also use a large tea ball, but the cheesecloth works better.

    1   (6-inch) square cheesecloth or tea ball
    1   tablespoon chopped fresh parsley with stems
    1   teaspoon dried thyme
    2   bay leaves
    1/2 teaspoon black peppercorns
    3   garlic cloves, minced
    4   whole cloves

❶ In cheesecloth, combine parsley, thyme, bay leaves, peppercorns, garlic and cloves. Bring corners together; tie with string.

1 bag.

CONFECTIONERS' SUGAR GLAZE

The perfect glaze everytime!

    1 1/2 cups powdered sugar
      1/4 cup melted butter
      1/4 cup heavy cream
        5 drops vanilla

❶ In large bowl, combine sugar and butter; mix well 30 seconds. Add cream and vanilla; mix until smooth. Beat 2 minutes at medium speed until smooth.

2 cups.

HOMEMADE NOODLES

Why spend hours creating something grand, and then diminish your results by using store-bought noodles? Here's my homemade alternative.

1¼ cups all-purpose flour
 1 egg
 5 egg yolks
 4 tablespoons melted butter
 1 tablespoon cold water
1½ teaspoons salt

❶ In large bowl, combine 1 cup of the flour, egg, egg yolks, 2 tablespoons of the butter, water and ½ teaspoon of the salt; stir with wooden spoon to make dough. Remove to lightly floured pastry cloth.

❷ Knead dough, working in remaining ¼ cup flour. (Do not over knead because the dough will become tough.) Cover with clean kitchen towel and let rest 30 minutes.

❸ Cut dough in half before rolling out. Roll out as if it were a pie crust, ¼ inch thick. Cut into thin strips with pizza cutter or sharp knife. Toss with small amount of flour to keep noodles from sticking together. Let dry 30 minutes.

❹ To cook, bring 2 quarts water and remaining 1 teaspoon salt to a fast boil. Add noodles and 1 tablespoon butter. Return to a boil and cook 15 to 20 minutes. Drain well. Add remaining 1 tablespoon butter, toss and serve.

4 servings.

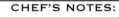

CHEF'S NOTES:
• Store uncooked noodles in tightly covered container and refrigerate. You can also freeze noodles, but don't thaw them before cooking.

Basic Recipes **15**

FISH RUB   *Pictured at right*

There is no salt in this recipe because salt draws moisture out of the fish. Salt should be added only after cooking. The rub will not tenderize fish.

- 1/2 teaspoon garlic powder
- 1/2 teaspoon white pepper
- 1/2 teaspoon dried thyme
- 1 tablespoon dried tarragon
- 1/2 teaspoon Hungarian paprika
- 1 teaspoon onion powder
- 1/4 teaspoon ground allspice
- 1/2 teaspoon ground brown mustard seeds
- 1/2 teaspoon dried dill weed
- 1 teaspoon lemon crystals
- 2 tablespoons vegetable oil

❶ In medium jar, combine garlic powder, pepper, thyme, tarragon, paprika, onion powder, allspice, mustard seeds, dill and lemon; cover and shake well. Rub mixture on fish fillets or fish steaks.

❷ Place fish in resealable plastic bag with vegetable oil at least 2 hours before grilling or sautéeing.

1/3 cup.

STEAK AND CHOP RUB

Do not put rub spices on too thick or it will get you a burnt crust.

- 2 tablespoons freshly ground pepper
- 2 tablespoons onion powder
- 1 tablespoon garlic powder
- 1 tablespoon Hungarian paprika
- 2 teaspoons dry mustard
- 2 teaspoons ground ginger
- 1 teaspoon ground allspice
- 2 tablespoons olive oil

❶ In large bowl, combine pepper, onion powder, garlic powder, paprika, mustard, ginger and allspice; blend well. Spread rub on steak or chops 30 minutes before grilling.

❷ Place steak or chops in resealable plastic bag with small amount of olive oil. This softens the spices and helps prevent a burned crust.

1/3 cup.

STICKY RICE

Short- and medium-grain white rice are cooked the same way.

- 2 cups long-grain white rice
- 1 teaspoon salt
- 4 cups water

❶ Heat oven to 350°F.

❷ Place rice in large bowl with enough water to cover. Stir rice with long-handled spoon. All rice hulls and bad kernels will float to top; remove floaters. Pour water and rice into strainer.

❸ Spoon rice into 8-inch square pan. In medium bowl, combine salt and 4 cups cold water; pour over rice. Cover pan with aluminum foil. Poke about 12 small holes into foil with pencil. Bake 1 hour or until water has evaporated and rice is tender and sticky. Remove foil; fluff rice with fork. For sticky rice, leave foil cover on when removed from oven.

4 servings.

BAKING POWDER DUMPLINGS

Dumplings are a lost art, and that's a shame because they're such a great side dish. For an interesting variation here, add 2 teaspoons fresh dill.

- 2 eggs, beaten
- 1/4 cup milk
- 1/2 teaspoon salt
- 2 tablespoons oil
- 1 cup all-purpose flour
- 1 tablespoon Cream of Wheat
- 2 teaspoons baking powder

❶ In large bowl, beat eggs at medium speed until frothy. Add milk, salt and oil; mix well. In another large bowl, combine flour, Cream of Wheat and baking powder. Gently combine with egg mixture.

❷ Dip spoon into boiling liquid. Dip spoon into batter and back into boiling liquid; batter will slide off spoon. Continue until batter is gone. Cover and simmer 12 to 15 minutes.

4 servings.

HOMEMADE BARBECUE DEMI-GLACE

Use any favorite barbecue sauce. I purchase a jug of moderately priced wine.

4 cups Burgundy wine
1 (18-oz.) bottle plain barbecue sauce
1/2 teaspoon white pepper

❶ In heavy saucepan, reduce wine to 2 cups. Add barbecue sauce and white pepper. Simmer over low heat 30 minutes.

❷ Strain through a fine strainer. Keep refrigerated.

12 servings.

CHEF JOHN'S HORSERADISH

Store-bought horseradish is a frail imitation of the real thing, often unnecessarily hot. Here's my alternative. To make horseradish hotter, add more white pepper and another jalapeño chile pepper.

5 cups shredded horseradish
1/2 cup cold water
1 1/2 cups white wine vinegar
1/2 teaspoon white pepper
1/2 cup sugar
1 jalapeño chile, stem and seeds removed, cut into 1/4-inch pieces

❶ In large bowl, combine horseradish, water, vinegar, white pepper and sugar; stir until thoroughly combined. Add chile; stir.

❷ Place in large covered container. Let stand unrefrigerated 3 days; stirring occasionally. Store in refrigerator.

2 cups.

> **CHEF'S NOTES:**
> • I like the texture of shredded horseradish, but you can chop it in a food processor or grind the horseradish, if you prefer.

GREAT MASHED POTATOES AND VARIATIONS

Here's my basic recipe for making Great Mashed Potatoes, *and then my variations (that I'd like you to try) for making them heavenly!*

4 to 6 russet potatoes, peeled or unpeeled
     1 tablespoon plus 1 teaspoon salt
   1/2 cup butter
   1/4 cup heavy cream
   1/4 teaspoon white pepper

❶ Rinse potatoes under cold water; cut into quarters. Place potatoes in large pot. Add enough cold water to cover potatoes; add 1 tablespoon salt. Heat to a boil. Reduce heat and boil until potatoes are tender when poked with thin paring knife; drain.

❷ Let potatoes stand uncovered 3 to 5 minutes, allowing liquid to steam off. Add butter, cream, remaining 1 teaspoon salt and pepper. Mash until creamy.

4 servings.

> **CHEF'S NOTES:**
> • It is better to undercook, rather than overcook, potatoes.
> • It is very important to drain off all water and let steam off 3 to 5 minutes before mashing.

ROASTED POBLANO CHILE AND CILANTRO MASHED POTATOES *Pictured at left*

   1/2 cup butter
   1/3 cup garlic cloves, peeled
     1 poblano chile, stem and seeds removed
     1 tablespoon finely minced fresh cilantro

❶ Heat oven to 325°F.

❷ Place butter, garlic and chile in small, covered, ovenproof pot. Bake 1 hour.

❸ In food processor, puree mixture to fine consistency. Add puree mixture to potatoes while mashing. When finished mashing, fold in cilantro. Puree can be prepared in advance; store in covered glass jar in refrigerator.

4 servings.

ROASTED GARLIC MASHED POTATOES

1/3 cup garlic cloves cut, peeled
1/2 cup butter

❶ Heat oven to 325°F.

❷ Place garlic cloves and butter in small, covered, ovenproof pot. Bake 1 hour.

❸ In food processor, puree mixture to fine consistency. If more liquid is needed to puree, add heavy cream, 1 teaspoon at a time. Add puree mixture to potatoes while mashing. Puree can be prepared in advance; store in covered glass jar in refrigerator.

4 servings.

COUNTRY MASHED POTATOES

1 1/2 cups sour cream
1/3 cup crisp crumbled bacon
1/3 cup thinly sliced scallions
1/8 teaspoon freshly ground pepper

❶ After potatoes are steamed off, add sour cream; mash. Fold in bacon, scallions and pepper.

4 servings.

CELERY MASHED POTATOES

1/2 cup butter
2 cups peeled sliced celery (1/2 inch)

❶ Heat oven to 325°F.

❷ Place butter and celery in covered ovenproof pot. Bake 30 minutes.

❸ In food processor, puree mixture to fine consistency. Add puree mixture to potatoes while mashing. Puree can be prepared in advance; store in covered glass jar in refrigerator.

4 servings.

POTATO DUMPLINGS

Potato Dumplings are another lost art that I refuse to let die, so I share my recipe here. I prefer fried dumplings and dumplings stuffed with meat, vegetables, cheese or fruit, so I'm including ideas for all these variations.

1	quart prepared *Great Mashed Potatoes* (**page 21**)
1	quart prepared *Seasoned Flour* (**page 9**)
1	tablespoon Cream of Wheat
1	teaspoon salt
1	cup cooked wild rice
1	egg, beaten
2 to 3	tablespoons melted butter

❶ Peel, boil and mash potatoes. Place cold mashed potatoes in large bowl with Seasoned Flour, Cream of Wheat, salt, wild rice and egg; mix by hand to combine. When thoroughly mixed, let dough stand 5 minutes. Shape into 10 (3-oz.) cylinder-shaped dumplings.

❷ Bring salted water to a boil in large pot; add dumplings. Stir gently to keep dumplings from falling to bottom of pot. Return to a brisk boil; cook 15 minutes.

❸ Check dumplings for doneness by slicing through center. Dumpling is cooked through when it appears fluffy and white throughout. Remove dumplings from water, make one slit in center of each; brush with butter.

❹ For fried dumplings (my favorite for breakfast), cut each dumpling into 4 slices; fry in butter until golden brown.

❺ For stuffed dumplings, make each dumpling 1/3 cup size. Roll into ball shape. Press hole into dumpling with your thumb. Fill hole with stuffing and reshape, covering up hole. Boil in salted water 15 to 20 minutes and serve.

10 dumplings.

SUGGESTED FILLINGS:

Meat: Diced ham, Canadian bacon bits, diced cooked Polish sausage, other cooked sausage meats, corned beef.

Vegetables: Onions, peppers, salted white cabbage, diced mushrooms, peas. Note: All vegetables should be precooked.

Cheese: Any kind, cut into small pieces.

Fruit: As a dessert, try filling with plums, apricots or spicy apples, and topping with *Confectioners' Sugar Glaze* (**page 14**).

POTATO PANCAKES

These pancakes are culinary poems. You can serve them as a main course at breakfast, as a late supper, or as a wonderful accompaniment to lunch or dinner.

3 to 4	potatoes, peeled, grated (1½ lb.)
1½	cups peeled grated onions
1	teaspoon lemon juice
1	egg
2	egg yolks
2	tablespoons bread flour
¼	cup Cream of Wheat
1	teaspoon salt
½	teaspoon freshly ground pepper
¼	teaspoon nutmeg
1	tablespoon chopped fresh parsley
1½	cups vegetable oil

❶ Heat oven to 375°F. In large bowl, combine potatoes, onions and lemon juice. Place in strainer; drain. Set potatoes aside; cover.

❷ Add egg and egg yolks to potatoes; mix well. In large bowl, combine flour, Cream of Wheat, salt, pepper, nutmeg and parsley; mix thoroughly. Add to potatoes.

❸ In large skillet, heat oil over medium-high heat until hot. For each pancake, pour ½ cup mixture into skillet; lightly press to about ½ inch thick. Cook until lightly brown, turning once.

❹ Place pancakes on baking sheet; bake until browned and crisp.

4 servings.

CHEF'S NOTES:

• If you prefer, you can fry the pancakes until they are browned and crisp, rather than baking them.

• If you are making potato pancakes in advance, it is best to finish them in the oven.

FARMERS' WIVES' JAM MADE WITH FRESH FRUIT OR BERRIES

This is an old farmers' wives' recipe from France. It's simple, but the results let the fruit or berries be the star attraction. And that is as it should be!

3 lb. fresh fruit or berries
4 cups sugar
1/4 cup lemon juice
1 cup water
1 teaspoon salt

❶ Fill clean sink half full of cold water. Add fruit; gently plunge up and down. Lift fruit from water, leaving debris in water. Place fruit in strainer. Remove any stems or pits. Peel fruit with sharp potato peeler. Cut fruit into 1-inch cubes. Leave berries whole.

❷ In large bowl, very gently combine fruit or berries with sugar and lemon juice. Cover and let stand overnight in refrigerator.

❸ Place fruit in colander to drain liquid into bowl; reserve liquid. Let stand 1 hour.

❹ Transfer reserved liquid to large saucepan. Add 1 cup water and salt; bring liquid to a boil over medium heat. Add fruit; stir gently with wooden spoon. Return to a boil; remove immediately from heat. Pour hot jam into shallow bowl or baking pan. Let cool on wire rack 30 minutes. Pour jam into glass jars or covered bowl. Store in refrigerator up to 2 weeks.

About 2½ quarts.

CHEF'S NOTES:

• Make sure to stir bottom of pot with a wooden spoon to keep from burning.

• Do not cook longer than the point of jam coming to a fast bubble.

• Make sure to scrape all sugar and juice from steeping bowl into colander.

• To can cooked jam, wash jars and lids and place in large pot covered with water. Bring to a boil. With tongs, remove jar and lids. Place on clean kitchen towel. Fill jars to the top with boiling jam. Top with lid and sealing ring. Tighten hand tight. Turn jars upside down and let cool. This will seal lids. The jam must be boiling hot, right from the pot.

GRANDMA SCHUMACHER'S HASH BROWNS

Only a grandmother could create hash browns as good as these.

  6 cups grated uncooked potatoes
  2 teaspoons fresh lemon juice
 1/2 cup diced onions (1/4 inch)
 1/2 cup heavy cream
  1 teaspoon salt
 1/2 teaspoon white pepper
 1/4 cup butter

❶ In large bowl, combine potatoes and lemon juice; let stand 10 minutes. Drain off excess liquid. Add onions, cream, salt and pepper to potato mixture; mix well.

❷ In medium skillet, melt butter over medium-high heat. Add potato batter; cover. Cook over medium heat until brown. Turn potatoes; cover and steam through. Potatoes should be light brown on both sides. Remove from pan; cut into squares.

4 servings.

> **CHEF'S NOTES:**
> • Be careful not to use too large of a skillet. Potato squares should be about 2 inches thick. If using an electric frying pan, cut potato cake in quarters before turning.

SCHUMACHER HOTEL SAUERKRAUT

This is one of the most popular accompaniments at my hotel restaurant. It is easy to prepare, and in a covered glass or stainless steel container, it will keep for 2 weeks in your refrigerator.

   2 lb. fresh or frozen (thawed) sauerkraut
  1/3 cup sugar
 11/2 tablespoons all-purpose flour
   2 teaspoons chicken soup base
  1/4 teaspoon white pepper
   2 teaspoons caraway seeds
 11/4 cups prepared *Chicken Stock* (page 8)

❶ Rinse sauerkraut in colander under cold water; drain.

❷ In large bowl, stir together sugar, flour and chicken soup base; mix well. Combine sauerkraut, sugar mixture, pepper, caraway seeds and Chicken Stock in large pot; stir gently.

❸ Bring mixture to a slow boil over medium heat. Stir and simmer 15 minutes.

4 servings.

> **CHEF'S NOTES:**
> • If you don't have Chicken Stock, you can substitute pork stock.
> • Kraut is made with salt and needs to be rinsed in cold water before cooking.
> • Prepare sauerkraut at least 2 to 3 hours in advance to allow flavors to fuse. Refrigerate, reheat and serve.

BEER-BATTERED FISH *Pictured at right*

Everyone can use a good recipe for fish, and I can't think of a better way than beer batter. This recipe works well because it does not contain salt. Salt will break down the frying oil, causing it to separate and burn.

    1   (12 oz.) bottle of beer
    1   cup all-purpose flour
    6   boneless panfish fillets or 4 (2x2-inch) fish squares
    1/4 cup prepared *Seasoned Flour* (page 9)
    1   quart vegetable oil

❶ Pour beer into large bowl. Add flour; whisk until smooth. Refrigerate until needed.

❷ Heat electric skillet to 375°F. Dredge fish pieces in seasoned flour, shaking off excess. Dip in beer batter, shaking off excess. Fry in oil until golden brown and fish flakes easily.

❸ Remove fried fish pieces to paper towel-lined bowl. Sprinkle with your favorite seasoning.

4 servings.

TARTAR SAUCE

This sauce goes very well with chicken and all upland fowl (such as pheasant), waterfowl and of course, fish.

    1   jalapeño chile, stem and seeds removed, diced (1/4 inch)
    3/4 cup diced dill pickles (1/4 inch)
    1/3 cup diced onions (1/4 inch)
    3/4 cup diced ripe olives (1/4 inch)
    2   cups mayonnaise
    1   tablespoon sugar
    1   tablespoon fresh lemon juice
    1   teaspoon tarragon leaves
    2   teaspoons mustard
    4   drops red pepper sauce
    1   teaspoon freshly ground pepper
    2   teaspoons Worcestershire sauce

❶ In strainer, drain pickles, onions and black olives.

❷ In large bowl, combine mayonnaise, sugar, lemon juice, tarragon, mustard, red pepper sauce, pepper and Worcestershire sauce; mix well. Gently fold in onions, pickles, black olives and jalapeño chile.

❸ Store in refrigerator. Keep tightly covered up to one week.

12 servings.

COOKING VEGETABLES

Working with vegetables isn't quite so simple as one might think. Here are some tips and insights for fresh, great flavor.

CLEANING FRESH VEGETABLES
- The best way to clean vegetables is to fill a sink or large bowl with cold water and add a generous amount of salt. Place vegetables in water and scrub with brush. Gently plunge vegetables. Remove from water and place in colander to drain.

BLANCHING GARDEN VEGETABLES
- To blanch vegetables, place 1 tablespoon salt, 1/4 cup sugar and 1/2 lemon in 1 gallon of water; bring to a boil. Add vegetables; return to a boil. As soon as water is boiling again, remove vegetables, drain and cool under cold water. Drain well. Keep refrigerated until serving.
- By blanching vegetables, you preserve their color and crispness. Now you can prepare them hot or cold.

PREPARING FRESH MUSHROOMS
- Fill large bowl with cold, salted water; place mushrooms in water. Swirl and wash mushrooms. Mushrooms are like sponges, so you cannot soak them. Remove mushrooms from water immediately; transfer to strainer and drain.
- To use as a raw vegetable, cut mushroom into quarters; splash with lemon juice. Cover until served.
- To use as a cooked vegetable, slice mushrooms about 1/4 inch thick; sauté in butter. Splash with white wine or sherry; serve.
- To use with other vegetables, sauté mushrooms separately. Add just before serving.

> **CHEF'S NOTES:**
> - If your mushrooms start to age, peel off their skins. This will make them whiter and more tender.

PREPARING RED, YELLOW AND GREEN BELL PEPPERS
- Clean, core, and seed peppers. Cut into desired shape, or leave whole for stuffing. Bring salted water to a boil; add peppers. Return to a boil. As soon as water is boiling, remove from heat. Drain and cool under cold water; drain well. All peppers should be blanched in this way; the blanching keeps the pepper flavor from overwhelming the flavors of the dish you are preparing.

HOW TO KNEAD BREAD

Everyone should know how to knead bread. Here's how I learned how to do it.

- Place dough on lightly floured bread board or pastry cloth.
- Fold dough over toward yourself; press down and away from you with the heel of your hand.
- Give dough a quarter turn and repeat until dough is smooth, elastic and doesn't stick. Most bread should be kneaded for 10 minutes.

Fold dough over and toward yourself.

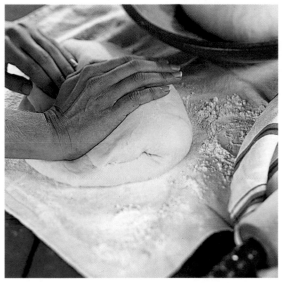

Press down and away with the heel of your hand.

FRESH BREAD CRUMBS

For different flavors, use whole wheat bread, light rye bread or pumpernickel bread.

1 to 1½   lb. loaf white bread

❶ Remove crust from bread. Cut slices in half. Place 4-half slices at one time into food processor; process into fine crumbs. Transfer crumbs to large bowl. Repeat until all crumbs are made. Making fresh bread crumbs is an important — and often overlooked — detail of cooking. Fresh bread crumbs are far superior to prepared crumbs, which become overcooked, dry and tasteless.

8 cups.

> **CHEF'S NOTES:**
> - Only make as many crumbs as you need.
> - Do not use leftover crumbs. You run the risk of food poisoning.
> - If crumbs are refrigerated too long, they will mold.

LUNCH

When I grew up, we ate not one lunch but three — at 10:00 or so in the morning, around 3:00 in the afternoon and then again about 9:00 in the evening. Lunch was a light "between meals" meal to keep you going. You might use these lunch recipes during the one lunch we eat today, or for an afternoon get-together, or as lighter fare for an evening meal.

Hard-Cooked Egg and Bacon Sandwiches, page 46

LEMONADE

There's lemonade, and then there's Lemonade! *Guess which one this is?*

LEMON BASE
- 2 cups sugar
- 1 cup freshly squeezed lemon juice
- Grated peel of 2 lemons

LEMON CUBES
- 1½ cups freshly squeezed lemon juice

LEMONADE
- ¼ cup lemon base
- 3 ice cubes
- 1 lemon cube
- 8 oz. cold water

❶ For Lemon Base, combine sugar, lemon juice and lemon peel in large saucepan; heat to a boil 3 minutes. Remove from heat; cool to room temperature. Store in refrigerator in covered glass container until served.

❷ For Lemon Cubes, freeze lemon juice in ice-cube tray. When frozen, transfer to resealable plastic bag.

❸ For 1 tall glass of Lemonade, combine base, cubes and water. As cubes melt, they keep each drink full of flavor. For pink color, add a little cranberry juice to lemon juice before freezing.

CHEF'S NOTES:

• The most important part of this Lemonade technique is to remove all white membrane from lemon peel with a potato peeler. The white membrane will make the Lemon Base bitter.

10 servings.

Preparation time: 10 minutes.
Ready to serve: 1 hour, 10 minutes.

Per serving: 165 calories, 0 g total fat (0 g saturated fat), 0 mg cholesterol, 10 mg sodium, 0 g fiber.

WHITE SUGAR COOKIES

Don't rely on a tube of dough from the supermarket when you want to bake up a batch of sugar cookies. This recipe makes the job easier — and the cookies better!

1/2   cup shortening
1/2   cup butter, softened
1   cup sugar
2   eggs
1   teaspoon vanilla
3   cups all-purpose flour
2   teaspoons cream of tartar
1   teaspoon baking soda
1/4   teaspoon salt
3   tablespoons heavy cream, whipped

❶ Heat oven to 375°F. Spray several baking sheets with nonstick cooking spray.

❷ In large bowl, beat shortening, butter and sugar at medium speed 2 minutes. Add eggs and vanilla; beat at medium speed until thoroughly combined. In large bowl, sift flour, cream of tartar, baking soda and salt; blend into shortening mixture with cream. Refrigerate at least 2 hours.

❸ Roll dough 1/8 inch thick onto flour-dusted bread board. Cut with 3-inch cookie cutter; arrange dough about 1 inch apart on baking sheets.

❹ Bake 6 to 8 minutes or until golden. Store cookies in airtight container.

4 dozen cookies.

Preparation time: 20 minutes.
Ready to serve: 1 hour.

Per serving: 90 calories, 4.5 g total fat (2 g saturated fat), 15 mg cholesterol, 55 mg sodium, 0 g fiber.

CHICKEN BREAST COBB SALAD

This salad works with all cooked fowl, not just chicken. Try turkey, a game hen, pheasant or quail too.

4	boneless skinless chicken breasts
1/2	cup all-purpose flour
1	teaspoon olive oil
1	tablespoon Worcestershire sauce
1	head iceberg lettuce
4	cups salad greens
1 1/2	cups cooked crumbled bacon
1	(11-oz.) can mandarin oranges, drained
4	hard-cooked eggs, crumbled
2	cups diced tomatoes
1	cup fresh blue cheese
1	cup sliced cucumbers

❶ Dredge chicken in flour; shake off excess. In large skillet, heat oil over medium heat until hot. Cook chicken over medium heat until no longer pink in center and juices run clear. Splash with Worcestershire sauce. Cut chicken into 3x1/2-inch strips; set aside.

❷ Remove inner leaves from head of lettuce to create "bowl". Place "bowl" on dinner plate. Combine remaining lettuce pieces with salad greens; fill lettuce bowl. Top with lines of bacon pieces, mandarin oranges, egg crumbles, tomato pieces, blue cheese and cucumber slices. Top with chicken strips. Or, serve on salad plate, as pictured.

4 servings.

Preparation time: 30 minutes. Ready to serve: 45 minutes.

Per serving: 840 calories, 49 g total fat (16.5 g saturated fat), 340 mg cholesterol, 1540 mg sodium, 6 g fiber.

CHEF'S NOTES:

• If you are not a blue cheese fan, use your favorite kind of cheese.

• My wife, Kathleen, likes sliced strawberries in this salad. Try them or some other fruit of your choosing.

FISH PAPRIKOSH

This recipe doesn't discriminate against other fish: You may also use haddock, halibut, lake trout, pike, catfish, perch or salmon.

1/4 cup butter
 2 garlic cloves, minced
 4 onions, diced (1/2 inch)
 2 teaspoons paprika
 1 teaspoon salt
1/4 teaspoon white pepper
1/4 cup sliced ripe olives (1/4 inch)
1/2 cup sliced mushrooms (1/2 inch)
1/2 cup chopped green bell pepper
1/2 cup dry red wine
1/3 cup water
1/2 cup tomato puree
 4 cups cod (or other fish) fillets, cut into 2-inch pieces

❶ Heat oven to 350°F. In large skillet, melt butter over medium heat. Add garlic and onions; sauté until onions are tender. Add paprika and mix. Stir in salt, pepper, olives, mushrooms, bell peppers, wine, water and tomato puree. Bring to a boil; reduce heat and simmer 10 minutes over low heat.

❷ Place fish in 3-quart casserole; top with onion mixture. Cover and bake 30 minutes or until fish flakes easily with fork. Top with sour cream and chopped parsley, if desired.

4 servings.

Preparation time: 30 minutes.
Ready to serve: 1 hour, 5 minutes.

Per serving: 485 calories, 30 g total fat (17 g saturated fat), 165 mg cholesterol, 1345 mg sodium, 4 g fiber.

CHEF'S NOTES:
• Serve this dish with fresh, homemade noodles, sautéed in butter and poppy seeds.

SCALLOPED POTATOES

No box here — just wholesome ingredients and full taste.

1/4	cup melted butter
1	cup sliced white onions (1/4 inch)
1	garlic clove, finely minced
2	teaspoons all-purpose flour
1	teaspoon salt
1/8	teaspoon white pepper
1/4	teaspoon nutmeg
6	cups peeled sliced potatoes (1/4-inch-thick rounds)
2	cups half-and-half

❶ Heat oven to 350°F. Spray 3-quart casserole with nonstick cooking spray.

❷ In large skillet, melt butter over medium heat. Add onion slices and garlic; cook until onions are transparent. (Do not brown.)

❸ Transfer to shallow bowl. Combine flour, salt, pepper and nutmeg; sprinkle over onion mixture. Toss gently to combine. Place 1 layer potatoes in casserole; top with one-third onion mixture. Build 3 layers and top with half-and-half.

❹ Cover and bake 1 1/4 hours or until potatoes are tender.

4 servings.

Preparation time: 15 minutes.
Ready to serve: 1 hour, 30 minutes.

Per serving: 450 calories, 26 g total fat (16 g saturated fat), 75 mg cholesterol, 720 mg sodium, 4.5 g fiber.

> **CHEF'S NOTES:**
> - Add one or more of the following if you wish, for an interesting variation:
>   - 1 cup frankfurters, cut into rounds.
>   - 1 cup corned beef cubed to 1/4 inch.
>   - 1 cup fresh mushroom caps cut into 1/4-inch slices.
>   - 1 cup whole kernel corn.
>   - 1 cup sea legs (crab-flavored fish).
> - If you substitute skim milk, the sauce will curdle.

STUFFED PEPPER VEGETABLE SANDWICH

Who says a sandwich needs meat to be good? This recipe, a favorite of mine, makes the point deliciously.

1/2 cup cooked pearl barley
4 cups vegetable juice
1 tablespoon Worcestershire sauce
1 teaspoon salt
1/2 teaspoon freshly ground pepper
3 garlic cloves, finely minced
4 large bell peppers
1/4 cup olive oil
2 onions, sliced (1/4 inch)
1 rib celery, sliced (1/4 inch)
1 cup sliced mushrooms (1/4 inch)
1 cup shredded cabbage (1/4 inch)
2 teaspoons dried basil
1 cup butter beans, drained

❶ Heat oven to 350°F.

❷ In 2-quart casserole, combine barley, 3 cups of the vegetable juice, Worcestershire sauce, salt, pepper and garlic. Cover with aluminum foil; poke about 12 holes in foil with pencil for steam to escape. Bake 45 minutes.

❸ Meanwhile, remove stem, seeds and pulp from bell peppers; dice stem end only of pepper. Set aside. In large skillet, heat oil over medium heat until hot. Add onions, celery and mushrooms. sauté until onions are transparent. Add cabbage and basil; cook until cabbage wilts. Let cool until barley is cooked.

❹ In large bowl, add cooked vegetables to barley mixture; combine well. Add drained butter beans and diced bell pepper.

❺ Fill individual peppers to top with barley mixture. Place remaining barley mixture in bottom of 8-inch square pan. Stand filled peppers on top of mixture. Pour remaining 1 cup vegetable juice over filled peppers.

❻ Cover and bake 30 minutes. Serve when peppers are hot and still a bit crisp.

❼ To serve hot, grill Kaiser roll or hard roll, if desired. Spread with thick layer of sour cream on both halves. Top with baked vegetable pepper.

❽ For salad, serve on large burger bun with lettuce and tartar sauce, if desired.

4 servings.

Preparation time: 20 minutes. Ready to serve: 1 hour, 50 minutes.

Per serving: 390 calories, 15 g total fat (2 g saturated fat), 0 mg cholesterol, 1405 mg sodium, 14 g fiber.

GERMAN POTATO SALAD

I get requests for this recipe all the time. It is a staple on our hotel's restaurant menu and a favorite dish all over central Europe.

9 medium potatoes (about 2 lbs.)
1/4 lb. thick-sliced bacon, cooked, crumbled
3 heaping tablespoons all-purpose flour
1 cup water
3/4 cup white vinegar
1/4 cup sugar
1 teaspoon salt
1/4 teaspoon white pepper
1/2 teaspoon celery seed
1/2 cup peeled thinly sliced onions
2 tablespoons diced red bell pepper (1/4 inch)
3 sprigs fresh parsley, finely chopped
1 tablespoon capers

❶ Boil potatoes until just tender, about 25 minutes; drain immediately. Let stand uncovered 3 to 5 minutes.

❷ In large skillet, cook bacon over medium heat until crisp. Add flour; cook 2 minutes, stirring to keep from burning. Add water and vinegar; mix well.

❸ In large bowl, combine sugar, salt, pepper and celery seed; add to bacon mixture, stirring frequently. Simmer 5 minutes over low heat.

❹ When potatoes are cool, peel and cut into 1/2-inch cubes; place in clean large bowl. Quarter onion slices; add to potatoes. Add bell peppers, parsley, capers and bacon mixture to bowl; stir gently to combine. Season with salt and pepper, if desired. Serve hot.

6 servings.

Preparation time: 45 minutes.
Ready to serve: 45 minutes.

Per serving: 250 calories, 3 g total fat (1 g saturated fat), 5 mg cholesterol, 970 mg sodium, 4 g fiber.

CHEF'S NOTES:
• This recipe will last in your refrigerator for about one week. It is a bit difficult to prepare, but once you have mastered it, you will make it again and again.

COUNTY FAIR CHILI CON CARNE

Con Carne is Spanish for chili with meat. It originates in Texas. Texans call it a "Bowl of Red." My mother made a chili like this for lunch for the first day of Minnesota's Traverse County Fair every September.

- 3 lb. beef round steak or roast
- 2 tablespoons olive oil
- 1/2 cup prepared *Seasoned Flour* (page 9)
- 1 1/2 teaspoons finely minced garlic
- 4 onions, diced (1/4 inch)
- 4 ribs celery, sliced (1/4 inch)
- 4 cups diced tomatoes
- 1 cup tomato puree
- 2 tablespoons beef base
- 1/4 cup chili powder
- 1/4 cup ground cumin
- 1/8 teaspoon Cajun pepper
- 1 teaspoon freshly ground pepper
- 2 teaspoons salt
- 2 cups drained chili beans, if desired
- 1 cup drained kidney beans, if desired

❶ Heat oven to 350°F.

❷ Remove excess silver skin and gristle from meat; slice 1/4 inch thick. Dice each slice into cubes.

❸ In Dutch oven, heat oil over medium heat until hot. Dredge meat in flour, shaking off excess. Add meat to oil; brown on all sides, stirring gently with wooden spoon. When browned, add garlic, onions and celery; cook 3 minutes, stirring frequently. Stir in diced tomatoes, tomato puree and beef base; mix well.

❹ In medium bowl, sift together chili powder, cumin, Cajun pepper, pepper and salt. Add to chili, mixing well.

❺ Cover and bake 1 hour or until beef is tender and no longer pink in center. Season with salt and pepper, if desired. Add beans during last 20 minutes of baking.

6 to 8 servings.

Preparation time: 30 minutes.

Ready to serve: 1 hour, 30 minutes.

Per serving: 320 calories, 8.5 g total fat (2 g saturated fat), 72 mg cholesterol, 1450 sodium, 7 g fiber.

HARD-COOKED EGG AND BACON SANDWICHES

From her farmhouse kitchen, my mother would bring this to us in the field for lunch.

- 1   teaspoon mustard
- 1/4   cup mayonnaise
- 1/2   teaspoon Worcestershire sauce
- 1/4   teaspoon salt
- 1/4   teaspoon freshly ground pepper
- 8   hard-cooked eggs peeled, chilled, sliced (1/4 inch)
- 1   cup peeled diced celery (1/4 inch)
- 1   cup cooked diced bacon (1/4 inch)
- 1/2   cup diced red onions (1/4 inch)
- 4   lettuce leaves
- 8   slices whole-wheat bread
- 2   tomatoes, sliced

❶ In small bowl, combine mustard, mayonnaise, Worcestershire sauce, salt and pepper.

❷ Place eggs in medium bowl; add celery, bacon and onions. Top with mustard mixture. Very gently fold together to combine. Keep egg slices as large as possible without breaking up. Salad will be on the dry side.

❸ To make sandwiches, pile egg mixture on top of garden lettuce on whole-wheat bread. Top with tomatoes and another slice of whole-wheat bread.

4 servings.

Preparation time: 15 minutes.
Ready to serve: 15 minutes.

Per serving: 530 calories, 33.5 g total fat (8.5 g saturated fat), 450 mg cholesterol, 1150 mg sodium, 5.5 g fiber.

CHEF'S NOTES:

• This mixture also makes a great dinner salad with fresh-baked sweet rolls.

• Sweet pickles are a tasty side. Or if you wish, dice them fine and add to the filling.

• Use your imagination for extra ingredients.

DINNER

On the farm, dinner was always at high noon. It was the main meal of the day, bridging the gap between a morning of hard work and the upcoming afternoon and evening of labor. Main dishes, side dishes, dessert — dinner was definitely the highlight of the culinary day. Treat your family to these delicious, hearty and wholesome recipes at any suitable time.

Roast Pork and Pan Gravy, page 61

SWISS STEAK

Made the right way, Swiss Steak *is superb, and this method can tenderize any piece of meat you consider a little tough. Here's how I do Swiss Steak.*

1/4 cup vegetable oil
  2 garlic cloves
  8 (4- to 6-oz.) cube steaks
  1 cup prepared *Seasoned Flour* (page 9)
  4 cups prepared *Beef Stock* (page 8)
  1 tablespoon beef soup base
  1 teaspoon freshly ground pepper
2 1/2 cups thinly sliced onions

❶ Heat oven to 350°F.

❷ In large skillet, heat oil over medium heat until hot; add garlic. Dredge cube steaks in Seasoned Flour; shaking off excess. Add steaks to hot oil, browning well on both sides. Transfer to 3-quart casserole.

❸ Add 1/4 cup flour to remaining oil; cook 1 minute, stirring constantly. Add Beef Stock, beef soup base and pepper; bring to a boil. Top steaks with onions and pan sauce.

❹ Cover casserole; bake 1 hour or until steaks are tender. Serve garnished with sour cream.

8 servings.

Preparation time: 25 minutes. Ready to serve: 1 hour, 40 minutes.

Per serving: 440 calories, 21 g total fat (6 g saturated fat), 85 mg cholesterol, 895 mg sodium, 1.5 g fiber.

CHEF'S NOTES:

• For a change of flavor, add 1 cup tomato sauce.

• You can also add 1 cup sliced mushrooms with the liquid.

• These cube steaks go well with cheese in a cold sandwich for lunch.

BOILED DINNER

This classic European dish is typically served on Sundays as a midday meal.

- 1/3 cup vegetable oil
- 1 (3- to 4-lb.) shoulder roast, bone-in
- 3 quarts water
- 3 garlic cloves
- 2 teaspoons caraway seeds
- 3 bay leaves
- 1 tablespoon beef soup base
- 2 teaspoons salt
- 1 teaspoon freshly ground pepper
- 1 head green cabbage
- 2 cups diced onions (1 inch)
- 2 cups sliced carrots (2 inches)
- 2 cups peeled sliced celery (2 inches)
- 6 to 8 small red potatoes, unpeeled

❶ In Dutch oven, heat oil over medium heat until hot. Add beef, browning on all sides. Transfer to large pot; add water, garlic, caraway seeds, bay leaves, beef soup base, salt and pepper; boil slowly 2¾ hours, skimming foam occasionally.

❷ Remove outer leaves from cabbage; cut into 6 wedges, leaving outer leaves in place to keep cabbage pieces intact. Add onion, carrots, celery and potatoes; simmer in soup pot until tender, about 30 minutes. Remove meat and vegetables; cut into bite-size pieces. Serve with *Chef John's Horseradish Sauce* (page 19) or hot German mustard.

8 servings.

Preparation time: 35 minutes. Ready to serve: 4 hours.

Per serving: 750 calories, 34 g total fat (10.5 g saturated fat), 125 mg cholesterol, 505 mg sodium, 13 g fiber.

CHEF'S NOTES:
• You can use corned beef, bone-in-ham or wild game in place of roast beef.

SATURDAY SOUP (BEEF, VEGETABLE AND BARLEY SOUP)

My mother makes this soup every Saturday on the farm. She has since the 1950s! She adds Baking Powder Dumplings *(page 18) the last 10 minutes of cooking.*

1	(3- to 4-lb.) game roast, boneless or bone-in
1/2	cup oil
2	cups onions, cut into 1-inch cubes
2	cups carrots, cut into 1-inch cubes
1	cup celery cut into 1-inch cubes
4	tomatoes, stems removed, cut into 1-inch cubes or 1 (16-oz.) can diced tomatoes
1½	cups pearl barley
3	bay leaves
1	teaspoon freshly ground pepper
2	teaspoons dried thyme
1	small head cabbage, cut into 1-inch cubes (about 6 cups)
1½	cups ketchup
1/4	cup Worcestershire sauce
1	gallon water
1/8	teaspoon salt
1/8	freshly ground pepper

❶ Remove excess fat and silver skin from roast. In Dutch oven, heat oil over medium heat until hot. Add roast; brown well on all sides. Transfer to clean plate.

❷ Add onions, carrots, celery and tomatoes to Dutch oven; sauté until onions are transparent, stirring frequently to keep from burning. Stir in pearl barley; cook 1 minute, stirring constantly. Add roast, spices, cabbage, ketchup, Worcestershire sauce and water. Cover and cook over medium heat, stirring occasionally, until meat is tender, about 1½ to 2 hours. Remove roast; cut into bite-size pieces. Remove and discard bay leaves. Return roast to soup. Season with salt and pepper.

6 to 8 servings.

Preparation time: 30 minutes.
Ready to serve: 2 hours, 15 minutes.

Per serving: 770 calories, 25 g total fat (5 g saturated fat), 190 mg cholesterol, 970 mg sodium, 15.5 g fiber.

CHEF'S NOTES:

• Do not worry if not all the ingredients are available. Just use what you have.

• It is important to use as heavy a covered pot as available. If using a thin or light pot to make the soup, be sure to cook over low heat for longer periods of time and stir often with a nonmetal spoon to keep barley from burning on the bottom.

EAT LOAF

If you prefer only beef, this recipe will work just as well. The pork is just added for some extra flavor. Make sure the internal temperature of the ground meat reaches 160°F. Use this same basic recipe to make Meatballs and Salisbury Steaks *(page 55).*

1½	lb. ground beef
1	lb. lean ground pork
½	cup prepared fresh whole-wheat *Fresh Bread Crumbs* (page 31)
2	cups cubed red onions (¼ inch)
2	teaspoons minced garlic
2	eggs, lightly whipped
½	cup tomato sauce
1	tablespoon Worcestershire sauce
1	teaspoon salt
1½	teaspoons freshly ground pepper

❶ Heat oven to 350°F. Spray 9x5x3-inch loaf pan with nonstick cooking spray.

❷ In large chilled bowl, combine beef and pork by hand until well mixed. Sprinkle Fresh Bread Crumbs, onions and garlic evenly over meat.

❸ In medium bowl, combine eggs, tomato sauce, Worcestershire sauce, salt, and pepper; pour over meat mixture. Mix by hand just enough to combine evenly. Cover and refrigerate 30 minutes.

❹ Mix one more time by hand. Press mixture into prepared pan. Press to remove any air holes. Bake until no longer pink in center, about 1 hour.

8 servings.

Preparation time: 20 minutes. Ready to serve time: 1 hour, 20 minutes.

Per serving: 345 calories, 21.5 g total fat (8 g saturated fat), 140 g cholesterol, 495 mg sodium, 1.5 g fiber.

> **CHEF'S NOTES:**
>
> • I add ½ cup of drained horseradish for a change of flavor.
>
> • For creamed meat, simply brown mixture in Dutch oven. Add mushroom sauce to thicken. You can also use canned soup for *Pan Gravy* (page 12).

Falling leaves, swirling winds, and a chill in the air — a great time for a brisk walk through the fields and a hearty meat loaf dinner.

MEATBALLS

Heat oven to 300°F. Scoop out meat from bowl with ice-cream scoop. Shape by hand into round balls. Roll in *Seasoned Flour* (page 9) and brown in skillet with 1 tablespoon vegetable oil 10 minutes. Place meatballs on baking sheet; bake 15 minutes or until no longer pink in center. Serve as is, or add your favorite sauce.

24 large meatballs.

SALISBURY STEAKS

Heat oven to 375°F. Divide meat into 6 large balls. Shape each into form of pear. Dust with flour. Place in 2-quart casserole; cover with chopped onions, 2 cups fresh sliced mushrooms and 3 cups *Pan Gravy* (page 12). Cover and bake until beef is no longer pink in center, about 30 minutes. Serve with 1/2 cup sauce per serving. These are excellent on hard rolls for lunch.

6 (10-oz.) steaks.

POT ROAST

Pot roast is another lost art, basic to country cooking, that I just won't let die. You shouldn't either. I make the largest roast I can for leftovers such as hot pot roast sandwiches.

1	(3- to 3½-lb.) boneless game roast
¼	cup vegetable oil
2	cups chopped onions (1 inch)
1½	cups chopped carrots (1 inch)
1½	cups chopped rutabaga (1 inch)
3	tablespoons all-purpose flour
⅔	cup dark raisins
2	teaspoons dried thyme
3	cups prepared *Beef Stock* (page 8)
½	cup dark rum
1	cup chili sauce
1	tablespoon beef base
⅓	cup molasses
1	teaspoon freshly ground pepper
1	cup red wine
1	tablespoon Worcestershire sauce
2	teaspoons cornstarch

❶ Heat oven to 350°F.

❷ Remove excess fat and silver skin from roast. In Dutch oven, heat oil over medium heat until hot. Add roast; brown on all sides, about 10 minutes.

❸ Add onions, carrots and rutabaga; cook until light brown, about 5 minutes. Add flour; cook 3 minutes, stirring constantly.

❹ Return roast to Dutch oven. Stir in raisins, thyme, Beef Stock, rum, chili sauce, beef base, molasses and pepper.

❺ Bake 2 hours. In small bowl, combine red wine, Worcestershire sauce and cornstarch to make smooth paste. Add to pot; stir to combine. Bake an additional 30 minutes. Remove meat; slice into thick pieces. Serve with vegetable sauce, if desired.

6 servings.

Preparation time: 30 minutes.
Ready to serve: 3 hours, 30 minutes.

Per serving: 595 calories, 16 g total fat (4 g saturated fat), 190 mg cholesterol, 660 mg sodium, 4.5 g fiber.

CHEF'S NOTES:

• It is important to brown the roast well to caramelize the meat sugars. This will add extra flavor.

Vomacka (Garden Vegetable Cream Soup)

We serve this traditional Czechoslovakian soup at my New Prague Hotel every Friday.

1/4 cup butter
1 cup diced onions (1/2 inch)
1 cup diced carrots (1/2 inch)
1 cup diced celery (1/2 inch)
3 garlic cloves, minced
1/4 cup all-purpose flour
6 cups prepared *Chicken Stock* (page 8)
1 tablespoon fresh dill
2 tablespoons chicken soup base
1/2 teaspoon black peppercorns
1 tablespoon pickling spice
3 cups cut green beans (1 inch)
3 cups diced potatoes (1/2 inch)
2 cups heavy cream, whipped
2 tablespoons cider vinegar

> **CHEF'S NOTES:**
> • You can add your favorite fresh vegetables for an excellent summer soup.
>
> • If you prefer a thicker soup, add mixture of 1/2 cup flour and 1/2 cup milk. Cook slowly 5 minutes.
>
> • To make Czech Booya, add veal, beef, venison, rabbit or squirrel. Simmer 2 hours.

❶ In large pot, melt butter over medium heat. Add onions, carrots, celery, and garlic; sauté until vegetables are tender and onions are transparent. Add flour; stir slowly and constantly with wooden spoon 2 minutes, eliminating lumps. Do not let mixture brown.

❷ Add Chicken Stock, dill and chicken soup base to pot. Place peppercorns and pickling spice into cheesecloth or tea strainer; add to sauce. Bring to a slow boil. Add beans and potatoes; simmer about 15 minutes or until tender. In saucepan, heat cream to a simmer; slowly add to soup. Remove pickling spice bag; stir in vinegar.

10 cups.

Preparation time: 30 minutes.
Ready to serve: 1 hour, 15 minutes.

Per cup: 480 calories, 35 g fat (20 g saturated fat), 110 mg cholesterol, 170 mg sodium, 5 g fiber.

COUNTRY PORK CHOPS IN BARBECUE SAUCE

This recipe is also excellent with a chicken cut into 8 pieces. Chicken must be cooked until internal temperature reaches 160°F. (Test the same as with pork chops.)

4 to 6	pork chops, bone-in (1 inch thick)
2	tablespoons vegetable oil
1/2	teaspoon freshly ground pepper
2	garlic cloves
2	onions, diced (1/2 inch)
3	tablespoons all-purpose flour
1	red bell pepper, diced (1/2 inch)
4	cups shredded green cabbage
1	cup barbecue sauce
1	cup prepared *Beef Stock* (page 8)
	Dash hot pepper sauce

❶ Heat oven to 350°F.

❷ Remove excess fat from pork chops. In Dutch oven, heat oil and pepper over medium heat until hot. Brown pork chops, two at a time, about 5 minutes per side. Set aside.

❸ Add garlic, onions and 1 tablespoon of the flour. Stir with wooden spoon to remove drippings. Cook onions until transparent, about 3 minutes. Add bell peppers and cabbage; cook 2 minutes. Stir well. In bowl, combine barbecue sauce, Beef Stock, remaining 2 tablespoons flour and hot pepper sauce; whisk until smooth.

❹ Add pork chops. Bake until no longer pink in center and juices run clear, about 1 to 1½ hours. Serve each pork chop with vegetables and *Homemade Barbecue Demi-Glaze* (page 19), if desired.

4 servings.

Preparation time: 15 minutes.
Ready to serve time: 1 hour, 30 minutes.

Per serving: 400 calories, 20 g total fat (5 g saturated fat), 90 mg cholesterol, 590 mg sodium, 3 g fiber.

> **CHEF'S NOTES:**
> • The reason to brown chops is to caramelize the sugar in the meat, for greater flavor.
>
> • For a spicier sauce, add 1 cup salsa of choice to Dutch oven during the last 20 minutes of baking.

ROAST BEEF HASH

I like my roast beef hash with poached eggs and rye toast.

 2   cups red potatoes, unpeeled
 1   tablespoon olive oil
 1½ cups roast beef cubes (¼ inch)
 1   cup diced red onions
 1   garlic clove, minced
 ½   teaspoon salt
 ½   teaspoon freshly ground pepper
 1   cup chili sauce
 ½   cup prepared *Homemade Barbecue Demi-Glace* (page 19)
 ½   cup diced dill pickles

❶ Boil and cool potatoes; cut into ¼-inch cubes. Heat oil in large skillet over medium heat until hot. Add roast beef; cook until browned and no longer pink in center. Stir in onions, garlic, salt and pepper. Cook until onion is tender.

❷ Add chili sauce, Homemade Barbecue Demi-Glace and pickles; bring to a boil. Reduce heat to medium; simmer 2 minutes. Add potatoes; cook until hot. Stir very gently and serve.

4 servings.

Preparation time: 35 minutes. Ready to serve: 45 minutes.

Per serving: 340 calories, 12 g total fat (3.5 g saturated fat), 40 mg cholesterol, 1815 mg sodium, 4 g fiber.

ROAST PORK AND PAN GRAVY

I can't lay claim to this classic recipe — it has been served consistently since 1898 at my New Prague Hotel. Over a century later, everyone still loves it. See this roast photographed full-page on pages 48-49.

ROAST

   1   (3- to 4-lb) fresh pork roast, boneless or bone-in
1½ cups water
1½ cups sliced onions (1 inch thick)
   1   teaspoon caraway seeds

GRAVY

   1 cup half-and-half
   1 cup hot water (120°F to 125°F)
 ½ cup prepared *Roux* (page 10)
 ⅛ teaspoon salt
 ⅛ teaspoon white pepper

❶ Heat oven to 275°F.

❷ Remove excess fat from roast. Place roast on rack in roasting pan; add water. Top roast evenly with onions and caraway seeds.

❸ Bake 4 hours or until internal temperature reaches 175°F.

❹ Transfer roast to holding pan. Remove rack from roasting pan. Remove onions from roast; place in pan with half-and-half and hot water. Stir with wooden spoon, scraping drippings from bottom of pan. Place pan on stovetop over low heat; bring liquid to a slow boil. Pour liquid through strainer into pan; return to a slow boil. Add Roux; whisk until smooth. Reduce heat to low; simmer 5 minutes. Season with salt and pepper.

6 servings.

Preparation time: 15 minutes. Ready to serve: 5 hours, 30 minutes.

Per serving: 430 calories, 25 g total fat (12 g saturated fat), 140 mg cholesterol, 180 mg sodium, 1 g fiber.

> **CHEF'S NOTES:**
>
> • For extra flavor in the gravy, add 2 teaspoons beef soup base with water/milk mixture.
>
> • My favorite hot sandwich is leftover pork heated in pork gravy with mashed potatoes or Czech dumplings. I've had at least one of these every week since 1974.

SUPPER

Probably eaten a little later than dinner, maybe mid-afternoon, supper for us was what you ate on a special occasion — a holiday, a Sunday dinner with family and maybe guests. Supper fare was a little "fancier" and "special" in the scheme of things. I'm sure you can think of situations in which to use these recipes, some of my all-time favorites.

Roasted Vegetables, page 70

BAKED STUFFED ONIONS

Onions are sweet, mild and flavorful when baked. This recipe makes them even better.

 2   quarts water
 1/3 cup cider vinegar
 4   (4-inch) onions, peeled
 2   teaspoons all-purpose flour
 4   teaspoons prepared *Fish Rub* (page 16)
 4   (4-oz.) boneless fish fillets
 2   tablespoons whole butter, softened
 1   cup prepared *Chicken Stock* (page 8)

❶ Fill large bowl half full of cold water; add 1/3 cup cider vinegar. Gently plunge onions up and down to clean; remove and set in Dutch oven, stem end down. Cut 1/4 to 1/2 inch off top. If onion will not set up straight, cut very thin slice off bottom. Remove onion center with melon ball scoop or teaspoon, being careful to leave 1/4 inch thickness on sides and bottom.

❷ Heat oven to 375°F.

❸ In shallow bowl, combine flour and Fish Rub. Coat each fish fillet; do not shake off excess flour seasoning. Roll each fillet into cylinder; place in center of onion, topping with soft butter. Place onion lid on top.

❹ Add Chicken Stock and onion pieces from centers into 11x7-inch baking dish. Cover and bake 55 minutes or until fish flakes easily with fork. Remove cover and bake an additional 20 minutes or until onion skins are crisp. Gently remove onions. Serve with polenta, risotto or spätzles.

4 servings.

Preparation time: 20 minutes.
Ready to serve: 1 hour, 15 minutes.

Per serving: 340 calories, 9 g total fat (4.5 g saturated fat), 140 mg cholesterol, 245 mg sodium, 3.5 g fiber.

CHEF'S NOTES:

• It makes no difference what color onions you use; only the size counts.

• Add vinegar to the cleaning water because the acidity helps kill bacteria.

• Popcorn shrimp, crabmeat or scallop slices placed inside the fish rolls adds great additional flavor to this dish.

• For a change, replace the fish with chicken. Just flatten a boneless skinless chicken breast and sauté until golden on both sides. Continue as directed, rolling the boneless breast into the center of an onion (step 3).

$\mathcal{B}$READED PORK CHOPS

This classic European dish is typically served on Sundays, as a midday meal.

8   eggs
1/2   cup freshly grated Parmesan cheese
1/3   cup prepard *Clarified Butter* (page 9)
8   center-cut pork chops (1 inch)
1   cup prepared *Seasoned Flour* (page 9)
2   cups prepared *Fresh Bread Crumbs* (page 31)
2   teaspoons fresh lemon juice
8   lemon slices (1/4 inch)

❶ Heat oven to 350°F. Spray baking sheet with nonstick cooking spray.

❷ In medium bowl, whisk together eggs and cheese.

❸ In large skillet, melt butter over medium heat. Dredge pork chops in Seasoned Flour, then dip in egg mixture. Dip in Fresh Bread Crumbs, coating well. Sauté pork to a light golden brown, about 3 minutes per side.

❹ Transfer pork to prepared baking sheet. Place 1/4 teaspoon lemon juice on each chop; bake until pork is no longer pink in center, about 25 to 30 minutes. Serve with lemon garnish.

4 servings.

Preparation time: 20 minutes. Ready to serve: 55 minutes.

Per serving: 761 calories, 43 g total fat (20 g saturated fat), 420 mg cholesterol, 1100 mg sodium, 1 g fiber.

CHEF'S NOTES:

• This recipe also works well with smoked pork chops or thick ham slices. Other garnishes could include mushroom sauce, tomato sauce or caper sauce.

• Cold leftover chops are best the next day for lunch or a snack.

CHICKEN FRICASSEE

I have replaced the batter in this traditional recipe with olive oil, and added more spices. The key to this dish is to keep the birds and sauce light.

1   (3- to 4-lb.) broiler-fryer chicken
1   cup all-purpose flour
2   teaspoons paprika
1   teaspoon salt
1/2   teaspoon white pepper
1   teaspoon poultry seasoning
1/4   cup olive oil
2   garlic cloves
2   cups prepared *Chicken Stock* (page 8)
4   whole shallots
8   carrot sticks, sliced (3 inches)
8   whole fresh mushrooms
2   cups half-and-half
1/4   teaspoon nutmeg
3   egg yolks
1   tablespoon cornstarch
1/2   cup sherry

❶ Heat oven to 350°F.

❷ Rinse and remove pin feathers, excess skin and fat from chicken. Cut chicken into 8 pieces (2 legs, 2 thighs, 2 breasts and 2 wings).

❸ In small bowl, combine flour, paprika, salt, pepper and poultry seasoning; mix well.

❹ In Dutch oven, heat oil over medium heat until hot; add garlic. Dip chicken pieces into Chicken Stock; dredge in flour to coat. Lightly shake off excess flour.

❺ Sauté chicken just until seared on all sides (do not brown); remove garlic. Stir 2 tablespoons flour mixture into olive oil. Do not break up chicken pieces. Add chicken dipping stock and shallots. Cover and bake 35 minutes. Add carrots and mushrooms. Return to oven and bake an additional 30 minutes or until chicken is no longer pink in center.

❻ In blender, combine half-and-half, nutmeg, egg yolks, cornstarch and sherry wine. Blend at low speed 20 seconds. Add one cup hot broth from base to temper liquid. Slowly add warm liquid to base. Cover and bake 20 minutes. Serve from Dutch oven.

4 servings.

Preparation time: 30 minutes.
Ready to serve: 1 hour, 30 minutes.

Per serving: 990 calories, 75 g total fat (31 g saturated fat), 420 mg cholesterol, 615 mg sodium, 2 g fiber.

> **CHEF'S NOTES:**
>
> • Two small fryers or large game hens cut in half are an excellent presentation.
>
> • I sometimes add ½ teaspoon lemon peel or 2 teaspoons fresh tarragon for a little extra flavor.

COCONUT LAMB CURRY

By all means, serve this dish with your favorite chutney. This is also an excellent way to prepare game with a wild taste you want to tame a bit.

1½ lb. lamb
½ cup *Seasoned Flour* (page 9)
2 tablespoons olive oil
2 garlic cloves, minced
2 onions, sliced (¼ inch)
1 cup coconut milk
3 teaspoons curry powder
1 (10¾-oz.) can cream of mushroom soup
1 cup prepared *Beef Stock* (page 8)
1 tablespoon beef soup base
1 teaspoon dry mustard
1 teaspoon freshly ground pepper
2 small jalapeño chiles, minced with seeds
½ cup chopped cashews
½ cup shredded coconut
1 tablespoon honey

❶ Heat oven to 350°F.

❷ Remove excess fat, silver skin and sinews from meat; cut into cubes. Dredge cubes in flour; shake off excess.

❸ In Dutch oven, heat oil to hot. Add lamb cubes; brown well on all sides. Transfer meat to platter. Add garlic and onions to Dutch oven; cook until tender. Add coconut milk, curry powder, soup, Beef Stock, beef soup base, mustard, pepper and jalapeño chiles; mix well. Add cooked meat. Cover and bake until tender, about 2 hours.

❹ In medium bowl, combine cashews and coconut; toss with honey to coat well. Spread out evenly into thin layer on baking sheet. Bake until golden brown, about 20 minutes. Remove from oven; let cool on pan.

❺ Serve curry over white rice topped with honey-coconut cashew pieces.

6 servings.

Preparation time: 20 minutes.
Ready to serve: 1 hour, 30 minutes.

Per serving: 710 calories, 50 g total fat (25 g saturated fat), 80 mg cholesterol, 1120 mg sodium, 5 g fiber.

CHEF'S NOTES:

• If you can't find coconut milk, use coconut piña colada mix.

• I line my baking sheet with aluminum foil for roasting nuts or coconut. This makes cleanup much easier.

ROASTED VEGETABLES

Roasting seems to capture and intensify vegetables' flavors, making them a sweet delight to eat versus the bland "blah" taste you get from steaming, boiling or (heaven help us) microwaving.

ROASTED CORN

8	ears sweet corn
2	quarts ice cold water
1/4	cup vegetable oil
1/2	lb. butter
1/8	teaspoon salt
1/8	teaspoon freshly ground pepper

❶ Remove corn silk (not husk). Place corn ears in water-filled container at least 20 minutes.

❷ Just before removing ears from water, add vegetable oil. Remove one ear at a time, allowing oil to coat husk.

❸ Heat grill. Place corn on gas grill over medium heat or on charcoal grill 4 to 6 inches from medium coals. Grill on each side 4 minutes. Turn ear one-third turn and repeat until all sides are roasted. Ears are ready when orange-yellow. Do not worry if husk becomes dark brown or black.

❹ To eat, peel husk back, cover corn with butter and sprinkle with salt and pepper.

4 servings.

Preparation time: 20 minutes.
Ready to serve: 40 minutes.

Per serving: 235 calories, 10 g total fat (5 g saturated fat), 20 mg cholesterol, 145 mg sodium, 4 g fiber.

CHEF'S NOTES:

• If you are taking corn on a camping trip or picnic, place corn in resealable plastic bag with ice. This will keep the corn cold and as the ice melts, the husks absorb the moisture.

• Do not put salt in the water for soaking, as salt will make the corn tough.

• After covering corn with butter, you may want to roll corn in a warm tortilla shell.

• For extra flavor, brush cooked corn with barbecue sauce, garlic butter, powdered cheddar cheese or Cajun seasoning.

• If you have corn left over, cut kernels from cobs with sharp knife and reserve. Reheat kernels in butter.

ROASTED SWEET PEPPERS

    4 whole bell peppers of choice
    2 tablespoons olive oil

❶ Wash peppers in warm water. Spray or brush olive oil over peppers.

❷ Heat grill. Place peppers on gas grill over medium heat or on charcoal grill 4 to 6 inches from medium coals. Cook peppers until light brown on all sides.

❸ Transfer to serving platter.

4 servings.

Preparation time: 15 minutes. Ready to serve: 40 minutes.

Per serving: 80 calories, 7 g total fat (1 g saturated fat), 0 mg cholesterol, 2 mg sodium, 1.5 g fiber.

ROASTED SUMMER SQUASH OR ZUCCHINI

    4 summer squash (green or yellow)
  1/4 cup olive oil

❶ Rinse squash in cold water; scrub with vegetable brush. Cut in half lengthwise; remove stem ends. Spray or brush squash with olive oil.

❷ Heat grill. Place squash on gas grill over medium heat or on charcoal grill 4 to 6 inches from medium coals. Grill 3 to 4 minutes; turn to mark. Grill 2 minutes; turn to cook bottom 2 minutes. Season with salt and pepper. Remove and serve 2 slices per person.

8 (1/4-squash) servings.

Preparation time: 12 minutes.
Ready to serve: 40 minutes.

Per serving: 75 calories, 7 g total fat (1 g saturated fat), 0 mg cholesterol, 3 mg sodium, 1 g fiber.

> **CHEF'S NOTES:**
> • Prepare acorn squash the same as you would summer squash, except remove seeds after cutting in half.

ROASTED CARROTS, PARSNIPS OR NEW POTATOES

8 carrots, parsnips or new potatoes
3 cups prepared *Chicken Stock* (page 8)
1 cup barbecue sauce

❶ Peel and remove ends from carrots or parsnips. In large pot, pour Chicken Stock and barbecue sauce over carrots, parsnips or potatoes. Simmer over medium heat 15 minutes. Remove from heat; cool.

❷ Heat grill. Remove vegetables from liquid. Brush or spray lightly with olive oil. Place vegetables on gas grill over medium heat or on charcoal grill 4 to 6 inches from medium coals. Grill until hot and golden brown on all sides.

4 servings.

Preparation time: 15 minutes.
Ready to serve: 40 minutes.

Per serving: 130 calories, 3 g total fat (.5 g saturated fat),
0 mg cholesterol, 215 mg sodium, 7 g fiber.

CHEF'S NOTES:

• For new potatoes, do not peel. Be sure to scrub with vegetable brush before cooking.

• The barbecue sauce in the Chicken Stock adds great flavor to the vegetables.

• Carrots, parsnips or potatoes should be simmered until half-cooked. They will continue to cook in the Stock after removing pot from heat.

• Keep the liquid stock for soup or for poaching other vegetables. This Stock is also excellent for precooking chicken or ribs before grilling.

• To take vegetables camping, after vegetables are cooked and well-chilled, place vegetables in a resealable plastic bag. Add ¼ cup olive oil to keep vegetables moist and coated in oil. Keep well chilled until time

$\mathcal{B}$ONELESS CHICKEN BREAST PARMESAN

For a hunter's style variation on this recipe, top the chicken with 1/2 cup mushroom sauce after baking.

4 eggs
3/4 cup freshly grated Parmesan cheese
1 cup prepared *Seasoned Flour* (page 9)
1/4 cup prepared *Clarified Butter* (page 9)
4 boneless skinless chicken breasts
2 tablespoons fresh lemon juice
8 (1/4-inch-thick) lemon slices

❶ Heat oven to 350°F.

❷ In medium bowl, whisk together eggs and cheese until smooth. Pour Seasoned Flour into large bowl.

❸ In large ovenproof skillet, heat butter over medium heat. Dredge chicken breasts, one at a time, in flour and egg mixtures. Dip chicken breasts back into flour. Place in skillet; sauté until golden brown. Turn; splash with lemon juice. Cover skillet; bake until chicken is no longer pink in center, about 40 minutes. Serve each portion with 2 lemon slices.

4 servings.

Preparation time: 15 minutes. Ready to serve: 45 minutes.

Per serving: 610 calories, 32 g total fat (15.5 g saturated fat), 540 mg cholesterol, 1700 mg sodium, 1 g fiber.

CHEF'S NOTES:

• For a tangy variation, place 1 1/2 tablespoons blue cheese on top of each chicken breast before placing in oven.

• It's important to only brown golden during the browning process, to keep breading from having a bitter taste.

THE FISHERMAN'S WIFE'S POT PIE

This recipe has a lot of ingredients and is some work, but it is well worth the time.

1/4 cup butter
1/2 cup diced red onions (1/4 inch)
1 cup sliced carrots (1/4-inch-thick half moons)
1/2 cup sherry wine
1 cup diced potatoes (1/2 inch)
1/2 cup diced mushrooms (1 inch)
1 cup chopped seeded tomatoes (1 inch)
1 cup cut fresh green beans (1 inch)
2 cups fish fillet pieces (1 inch)
4 cups heavy cream, whipped
3 egg yolks
1/4 teaspoon nutmeg
1/2 teaspoon salt
1/4 teaspoon white pepper
1 teaspoon fresh thyme or 1/2 teaspoon dried
2 teaspoons fresh tarragon or 1 teaspoon dried
1/4 cup all-purpose flour
1 recipe prepared *Pie Crust* (page 10)

❶ Heat oven to 350°F.

❷ In large skillet, melt butter over medium heat. Add onions and carrots; sauté 3 minutes, stirring gently to keep from sticking. Add sherry and potatoes; reduce heat to low and simmer 10 minutes. Remove from heat. Add mushrooms, tomatoes and green beans.

❸ Place mixture in 3-quart casserole; top with fish pieces.

❹ In large bowl, combine cream, egg yolks, nutmeg, salt, pepper, thyme, tarragon and flour; pour over fish. Top with pastry crust. Seal crust to edges of dish. Cut small vent in center to remove steam. Brush crust evenly with cream to enhance browning. Bake 1 hour or until pastry is golden brown.

4 servings.

Preparation time: 45 minutes.
Ready to serve: 1 hour, 45 minutes.

Per serving: 1260 calories, 105 g total fat (60 g saturated fat), 500 mg cholesterol, 700 mg sodium, 4.5 g fiber.

CHEF'S NOTES:

• You may use different kinds of fish pieces, or shrimp or scallops, in this dish.

• Make sure to use heavy cream, or the sauce will curdle.

ROAST CAPON AND GRAVY

I am not a fan of chicken skin so I just let the bird roast in the bag until the internal temperature reaches 180°F, and remove the skin before slicing.

1   (3- to 4-lb.) roasting chicken
1   teaspoon salt
1   tablespoon lemon juice
1   small lemon
1/4 teaspoon freshly ground pepper
2   sprigs fresh thyme
1   medium onion, chopped
1   cup sliced carrots (1/4 inch)
1   cup sliced celery (1/4 inch)
2   ribs celery, sliced (1/4 inch)
2   garlic cloves
2   tablespoons vegetable oil
1   cup half-and-half
1   cup hot water
1/2 cup prepared *Roux* (page 10)

❶ Remove giblets. Place thawed chicken and giblets into cold water, salt and lemon juice 15 minutes. Remove excess skin, fat and pin feathers from bird. Rinse well inside and out with cold water.

❷ Place whole lemon, pepper, thyme and one-half the vegetables inside chicken. Place chicken, giblets and remaining vegetables in roasting bag in roasting pan; insert thermometer. Bake 3 hours at 275°F until internal temperature reaches 180°F. Cut open bag to expose bird. Spray or brush skin with vegetable oil. Increase temperature to 350°F; bake 15 minutes to brown skin. Remove vegetables and lemon from cavity; transfer chicken to platter. Cover with plastic wrap; top with kitchen towel to keep warm.

❸ Discard lemon. Place all vegetables, liquid and giblets (except liver) in medium saucepan. Slowly add half-and-half and hot water; bring to a simmer. Strain liquid into large pot. Bring to a simmer; whisk in Roux. Return to a simmer; cook 3 to 4 minutes or until thickened. Discard vegetables; add giblets to roasted bird. Slice and serve with pan gravy.

6 servings.

Preparation time: 30 minutes. Ready to serve: 3 hours.

Per serving: 560 calories, 38 g total fat (17 g saturated fat), 180 mg cholesterol, 210 mg sodium, .25 g fiber.

SPARERIBS AND SAUERKRAUT

If you like, substitute a 2½ to 3 pound fryer chicken cut in half, to replace the spareribs. Chicken takes less baking time.

SPARERIBS

4	(2 to 2½ lb.) flat baby spareribs
¼	cup vegetable oil
1	teaspoon salt
½	teaspoon freshly ground pepper
4	cups prepared *Schumacher Hotel Sauerkraut* (page 27)

❶ Heat oven to 350°F. Remove tissue from inside of ribs. Brush both sides of ribs with vegetable oil; season with salt and pepper.

❷ Arrange ribs in 13x9-inch pan. Bake about 30 minutes, turning once, until thoroughly browned on both sides. Remove to Dutch oven.

❸ Spread Schumacher Hotel Sauerkraut over ribs. Cover tightly. Bake about 1½ hours or until ribs separate easily with fork.

❹ When rib bone turns easily, ribs are tender. Remove from oven and serve with boiled potatoes and rye bread.

4 servings.

Preparation time: 20 minutes.

Ready to serve: 1 hour, 30 minutes.

Per serving: 1645 calories, 120 g total fat (41.5 g saturated fat), 430 mg cholesterol, 2830 mg sodium, 7 g fiber.

CHEF'S NOTES:

• I prepare veal and pork shank this way, except I brown the shanks first in hot oil and remove any excess sinew or skin.

• It is difficult to estimate the proper baking time for this dish because of the difference in ribs and ovens. After the first 1½ hours, check every 15 minutes for tenderness.

VENISON SAUERBRATEN

Venison is really best for this old German recipe, but beef is also excellent to use if you don't know a generous hunter, or don't have a source for game farm venison. Pork may get a little dry, so I stay away from it in this case.

MARINADE
- 2½ cups prepared cold *Beef Stock* (page 8)
- 1½ cups red wine vinegar
- 1 cup Burgundy wine
- 1 cup thinly sliced onions
- ½ cup thinly sliced carrots
- ½ cup thinly sliced celery
- 2 tablespoons packed brown sugar
- 2 garlic cloves, minced
- ½ tablespoon salt
- 2 bay leaves
- 6 crushed black peppercorns
- 4 whole cloves
- 1 tablespoon juniper berries

MEAT
- 4 lb. venison
- ⅓ cup vegetable oil
- ⅔ cup crushed gingersnap cookies
- ⅔ cup raisins

❶ Heat oven to 375°F.

❷ In large container, combine Beef Stock, vinegar, wine, onions, carrots, celery, brown sugar, garlic, salt, bay leaves, peppercorns, cloves and berries; stir well. Pierce meat at random with boning knife. Add meat to marinade, covering completely. Place in covered container; marinate in refrigerator 72 hours. (If you marinate less than 72 hours, meat will be tough. If you marinate more than 72 hours, meat will become dry and flavorless.)

❸ Remove meat from marinade; wipe dry with clean kitchen towel. In large skillet, heat oil over medium heat until hot; brown meat. Transfer meat to Dutch oven. Pour marinade over meat. Bake, covered, 2½ hours or until tender. When meat is done, transfer to dry saucepan. Cover with damp cloth and keep warm.

❹ Remove and discard bay leaves. Puree liquid and vegetables in blender. Place in large pot; whisk crushed gingersnaps into liquid, stirring until smooth. Add raisins. Simmer 5 minutes. Cut meat across grain; serve with 2-oz. ladle of sauce per portion.

16 servings.

Preparation time: 72 hours. Ready to serve: 76 hours.

Per serving: 240 calories, 8 g total fat (2 g saturated fat), 95 mg cholesterol, 315 mg sodium, .75 g fiber.

> **CHEF'S NOTES:**
> • You may freeze meat and sauce separately.
>
> • To reheat cut meat, add to cold sauce and bake 45 minutes at 350°F.

SHRIMP WRAPPED IN COUNTRY BACON

This is such an easy recipe — sure to please both you and your guests. You can prepare this dish easily on an outside grill. You can also use large sea scallops instead of the shrimp.

20 large shrimp
10 strips lean bacon
 1 cup prepared *Homemade Barbecue Demi-Glace* (page 19)
 1 lemon

❶ Peel shrimp, leaving tails on. Cut bacon strips in half crosswise; wrap around center of each shrimp. Secure bacon and shrimp with toothpick.

❷ Place wrapped shrimp on broiler pan; brush with Homemade Barbecue Demi-Glace. Broil until one side is brown. Turn and brown other side until bacon is crisp and shrimp is pink; remove toothpick. Serve with lemon wedge.

> **CHEF'S NOTES:**
> • Both shrimp and scallops can also be placed on a long skewer with the bacon, especially if you are using a grill.

4 servings.

Preparation time: 20 minutes.
Ready to serve: 40 minutes.

Per serving: 155 calories, 8.5 g total fat (3 g saturated fat), 80 mg cholesterol, 585 mg sodium, 1 g fiber.

GRILLED ACORN SQUASH

Here's a baked squash recipe like you've never seen (or tasted) before!

4 (2-lb.) acorn squash
1 cup shredded cheddar cheese
2 cups cooked crabmeat or fish sea legs
1 cup teriyaki sauce

❶ Rinse squash under cold water; scrub with vegetable brush. With apple corer, remove 1-inch plug from stem end of squash. Scrape out seeds with salted water. Repeat until all seeds are removed.

❷ Heat grill. Insert cheese, crabmeat and teriyaki sauce through hole into squash. Replace plug. Place squash on gas grill over medium heat or on charcoal grill 4 to 6 inches from medium coals. Cook 45 minutes until squash is tender. If baking, heat oven to 375°F. Spray 13x9-inch pan with nonstick cooking spray; bake squash 1 hour.

4 servings.

Preparation time: 20 minutes.

Ready to serve: 1 hour, 30 minutes.

Per serving: 485 calories, 11 g total fat (6 g saturated fat), 100 mg cholesterol, 3140 mg sodium, 14 g fiber.

CHEF'S NOTES:

• When removing seeds from squash, it may take 2 to 3 rinsings with water to remove all the seeds. Don't worry if a few seeds are left inside the cavity.

• Any meat or fowl must be pre-cooked before adding to the cavity of the squash.

• Place squash plug-side-up when cooking.

• Use peach teriyaki sauce, if possible.

• For a new and exciting dessert, mix 2 cups applesauce with 1 cup brown sugar, 2 tablespoons soft butter and ½ teaspoon cinnamon. Put inside squash and bake 1 hour.

SATURDAY BAKING

Saturday was for baking, and it produced enough volume to last a hardworking and hungry family until the next Saturday. Bread was at the top of the list — loaf upon loaf, and different varieties. But "good stuff" was also made — three cakes, a couple batches of cookies, tea rolls and caramel rolls. Here are the recipes. The secret ingredient is a little love.

Card Club Sponge Cake, page 92

GRANDMA SCHUMACHER'S WHITE BREAD AND ROLLS

As a kid, my mother made this recipe once a week.

1/2	cup butter
1/2	tablespoon salt
1/2	cup sugar
1	cup milk
2	cups cold water
1 1/2	tablespoons active dry yeast
1/2	cup warm water (105°F to 115°F)
11	cups all-purpose flour
2	eggs, beaten slightly

❶ In large saucepan, heat butter, salt, sugar and milk over medium heat, stirring constantly until butter melts. Remove from heat; stir in 2 cups cold water.

❷ In small bowl, combine yeast and 1/2 cup warm water. Let set 1 minute.

❸ In large bowl, combine butter mixture and 3 cups of the flour; add yeast mixture and eggs, mixing well. Add another 8 cups flour, two cups at a time. After each addition, mix 1 minute. Place dough on top of pastry cloth; let rest 5 minutes. Knead until smooth, elastic and small bubbles appear, about 10 minutes.

❹ Place dough in greased large bowl, turning dough over to grease top. Cover with kitchen towel and let rise in warm place about 1 to 1 1/2 hours or until doubled in size. Punch down dough; let rise again. Divide into thirds. Cover with kitchen towel and let rest 5 minutes. Shape dough into 3 loaves; place into 3 (9x5x3-inch) loaf pans. Cover and let rise about 1 hour or until doubled again.

❺ Heat oven to 375°F. Bake 45 minutes or until loaves are golden brown. Remove from pans; cool on wire racks away from drafts.

3 (16-slice) loaves.

Preparation time: 45 minutes. Ready to serve: 5 hours.

Per slice: 140 calories, 2.5 g total fat (1 g saturated fat), 15 mg cholesterol, 90 mg sodium, 1.5 g fiber.

$\mathcal{B}$READ AND BUTTER APPLE CAKE

This is cake the way I like it — simple to make and eye-rolling delicious to eat. Give it a try on both counts.

  6 cups peeled sliced apples (¹⁄₄-inch wedges)
  1 cup sugar
  1 loaf raisin bread, sliced
¹⁄₂ cup butter
1¹⁄₂ cups strawberry jam
¹⁄₂ teaspoon nutmeg
¹⁄₂ teaspoon cinnamon
¹⁄₂ cup slivered almonds

❶ Heat oven to 375°F. Spray 12-cup Bundt pan with nonstick cooking spray; lightly flour.

❷ Spread bread slices with soft butter and 1 tablespoon jam. Arrange slices in single layer in pan, pressing up sides.

❸ In large bowl, combine apples, sugar, spices and almond slices; toss to combine, being careful not to break up apple slices.

❹ Place one-half of the apple mixture over bread lining. Top with layer of butter and jam bread slices. Add remaining apples; top with another second layer of butter and jam bread slices (spread sides down). Butter top of bread; bake 45 minutes.

❺ Invert pan onto serving plate; do not remove Bundt pan. After 15 minutes, remove pan; serve with homemade ice cream or whipped cinnamon cream, if desired.

16 servings.

Preparation time: 20 minutes.
Ready to serve: 1 hour, 30 minutes.

Per serving: 300 calories, 9 g total fat (4 g saturated fat), 15 mg cholesterol, 160 mg sodium, 3 g fiber.

$\mathcal{D}$OUBLE CHOCOLATE CAKE

Those of us who love chocolate know — double the chocolate and the cake DOES get doubly better!

CAKE
- 3/4 cup butter
- 1/2 teaspoon salt
- 2 teaspoons vanilla
- 2¼ cups sugar
- 3 eggs
- 3 (1-oz.) squares unsweetened chocolate
- 2½ cups cake flour
- 3/4 teaspoon baking powder
- 1½ teaspoons baking soda
- 1¼ cups cold water
- 1/4 cup crème de cocoa

FROSTING
- 1½ cups packed brown sugar
- 1 tablespoon crème de cocoa
- 1/4 cup butter
- 1 cup semisweet chocolate chips (6 oz.)
- 6 tablespoons heavy cream, whipped

❶ Heat oven to 350°F. Spray 13x9-inch pan with nonstick cooking spray; lightly flour.

❷ In large bowl, beat together butter, salt, vanilla and sugar at medium speed 3 minutes. Add eggs, one at a time, beating 20 seconds after each addition.

❸ Melt chocolate in double boiler or microwave. Add slowly to batter; beat 30 seconds.

❹ In another large bowl, sift together flour, baking powder and baking soda; add alternately with cold water and crème de cocoa. Beat 1 minute; pour batter into pan.

❺ Bake 40 to 45 minutes or until toothpick inserted near center comes out clean. Let cool on wire rack before frosting.

❻ To prepare frosting, boil brown sugar, crème de cocoa and butter in medium pot 1 minute. Add chocolate chips and cream; stir until melted and smooth. Cool; spread over cake.

12 servings.

Preparation time: 20 minutes. Ready to serve: 40 minutes.

Per slice: 660 calories, 28 g total fat (17 g saturated fat), 105 mg cholesterol, 430 mg sodium, 2.5 g fiber.

CARAMEL ROLLS

These rolls are unforgettable. Enjoy!

   1   recipe prepared *Grandma Schumacher's White Bread* (page 84)
 1/2   cup butter
   1   cup packed brown sugar
 1/2   cup heavy cream, whipped
 3/4   cup chopped pecans

❶ Spray 14x10-inch pan with nonstick cooking spray.

❷ Prepare dough for Grandma Schumacher's White Bread. After first
rise, roll dough out to 20x24-inch rectangle on floured pastry cloth,
making sure to keep corners square. Lightly roll up dough beginning
with top edge; tightly fasten edges. Cut into 2-inch slices with sharp
knife. Cover with kitchen towel and set in warm area until doubled in
size.

❸ In medium pan, melt butter over medium-high heat. Remove from
heat; stir in brown sugar and cream until mixture is smooth. Add
pecan pieces. Place mixture in pan; top with rolls. (Rolls should be
about
2 1/2 oz. each or 2 inches high.) Cover with kitchen towel and set in
warm area until doubled in size.

❹ Heat oven to 375°F. Bake 25 to 30 minutes or until golden brown.
Remove from oven; turn upside down on aluminum foil.

2 dozen rolls.

Preparation time: 45 minutes. Ready to serve: 5 hours.

Per roll: 260 calories, 9 g total fat (4 g saturated fat), 30 mg cholesterol, 145 mg sodium, 1.5 g fiber.

INNAMON ROLLS

You don't need a bakery to make great sweet rolls. Let this simple recipe show you why.

BREAD
- 1 recipe prepared *Grandma Schumacher's White Bread* (page 84)
- 1 egg
- 1 tablespoon heavy cream
- 1½ cups packed brown sugar
- 1 tablespoon cinnamon

GLAZE
- 1½ cups powdered sugar
- ¼ cup melted butter
- ¼ cup heavy cream
- 5 drops vanilla

❶ Spray 14x10-inch pan with nonstick cooking spray.

❷ Prepare dough for Grandma Schumacher's White Bread. After first rise, roll dough out to 20x24-inch rectangle on floured pastry cloth, making sure to keep corners square.

❸ In large bowl, beat egg and cream together at medium speed; brush evenly over dough. Sprinkle brown sugar and cinnamon evenly over dough, leaving 1-inch clean strip on bottom (to make tight seal). Lightly roll up dough beginning with top edge; tightly fasten edges. Cut into 2-inch slices with sharp knife. Arrange cut-side down in pan. Cover with kitchen towel and set in warm area until doubled in size.

❹ Heat oven to 375°F. Bake rolls 25 to 30 minutes or until golden brown. Remove from oven; invert onto wire rack or aluminum foil. Frost with glaze.

❺ To prepare glaze, sift powdered sugar. In large bowl, combine sugar and butter; beat at medium speed 30 seconds. Add cream and vanilla; beat at medium speed until smooth, about 2 minutes. Spread over rolls.

2 dozen rolls.

Preparation time: 45 minutes. Ready to serve: 5 hours.

Per roll: 340 calories, 5.5 g total fat (3 g saturated fat), 38 mg cholesterol, 195 mg sodium, 2 g fiber.

APPLE STRUDEL AM WIEN

This is one of the most difficult recipes in this cookbook, requiring care at each step. But after a few times, you will be as expert as a Viennese baker!

DOUGH
- 1/8 cup each melted butter, warm water
- 1 beaten egg
- 1 1/2 teaspoons sugar
- 1/8 teaspoon salt
- 1/2 teaspoon vanilla
- 1 1/2 cups all-purpose flour

FILLING
- 1 cup crushed corn flakes, moistened with 2 tablespoons melted butter
- 3/4 cup prepared *Fresh Bread Crumbs* (page 31)
- 6 cups apples, peeled, diced (1/4 inch)
- 3/4 cup raisins
- 3/4 cup walnut pieces
- 1 cup packed brown sugar
- 1/2 teaspoon cinnamon
- 1/2 cup snow-flaked coconut

❶ Heat oven to 350°F. Spray 2 (15x10x1-inch) baking sheets with nonstick cooking spray.

❷ To make dough, combine butter, water, egg, sugar, salt and vanilla in large bowl; mix well. Add flour to make soft but not sticky dough. Knead well (about 150 times). Place in greased covered bowl in warm area one hour. Roll out onto floured pastry cloth, stretching very thin. Form dough into 18x12-inch rectangle. Cut into 2 (9x12-inch) rolls.

❸ To make strüdel, layer corn flakes, Fresh Bread Crumbs, apples, raisins, walnuts, sugar, cinnamon and coconut onto rolled out dough in order listed. Dampen edge of crust with egg wash or water; roll up. Even out roll and place on baking sheets "seam" side down. Grease roll with melted butter. Bake until golden brown, about 50 minutes.

❹ Frost immediately with mixture of 1/3 cup powdered sugar and 1/3 cup whipped cream, if desired. Cool completely and slice.

6 servings.

Preparation time: 40 minutes. Ready to serve: 2 hours.

Per serving: 625 calories, 21 g total fat (8 g saturated fat), 55 mg cholesterol, 220 mg sodium, 5.5 g fiber.

CARD CLUB SPONGE CAKE

It is fun to make this cake. It is easy and takes only a few minutes to make the batter ... perfect for the old-fashioned "card club night" so many of us used to look forward to each week.

CAKE
- 1 cup half-and-half
- 2 tablespoons butter
- 5 eggs
- 2 cups sugar
- 1/2 teaspoon salt
- 1 tablespoon vanilla
- 2 cups sifted cake flour
- 2 teaspoons baking powder

FILLING
- 2 tablespoons freshly grated lemon peel
- 1 cup sugar
- 1/4 cup cornstarch
- 1/2 teaspoon salt
- 1 cup club soda
- 1/2 cup freshly squeezed lemon juice
- 2 tablespoons butter
- 1 teaspoon vanilla
- 1/4 cup heavy cream

TOPPING
- 1 (16-oz.) container whipped cream

❶ Heat oven to 350°F. Spray 2 (9-inch) pans with nonstick cooking spray; lightly flour.

❷ In large pot, heat half-and-half and butter to a low boil. Remove from heat.

❸ Separate eggs, placing 5 whites in large bowl. Place 4 yolks in small bowl; set aside. Discard fifth yolk. Add 1 cup of the sugar to egg whites; beat until mixture forms soft peaks. Gradually add remaining 1 cup sugar and 1/2 teaspoon salt, beating at highest speed until stiff peaks form.

❹ Add vanilla to hot half-and-half and butter mixture in large pot. With mixer at medium speed, add hot liquid to egg mixture in slow, even stream. Reduce speed to low. Immediately beat in cake flour and baking powder until lumps disappear.

❺ Pour batter into prepared pans. Bake 25 to 30 minutes or until toothpick inserted near center comes out clean. Let cool on baking rack 15 to 20 minutes. Place generous amount of granulated sugar on clean pastry cloth. Invert cake onto sugar; let cool.

❻ To prepare Filling, combine 1 tablespoon of the grated lemon peel, cup sugar, cornstarch, 1/2 teaspoon salt, club soda, lemon juice, butter and vanilla in blender; process 30 seconds. Transfer to large saucepan. Heat saucepan over medium heat. Bring mixture to a rolling boil, stirring often with wooden spoon to keep from scorching. Reduce heat to low.

❼ In small bowl of egg yolks, beat yolks and cream at low speed until mixture is thick and lemon colored. Remove 1/2 cup hot filling from large pot; slowly add to egg mixture. Stir to temper eggs. Slowly add warm mixture to base; stir until smooth. Simmer an additional 1 to 2 minutes. Pour cooked filling into large bowl; cover with plastic wrap. Poke 12 holes into plastic with toothpick to release heat and steam. Refrigerate until filling has thickened, about 1 hour.

❽ To assemble, top with one layer of Filling. Add second cake layer on top of filling. Cover cake with whipped cream.

4 to 6 servings

Preparation time: 20 minutes. Ready to serve: 2 hours.

Per serving: 780 calories, 25 g total fat (13 g saturated fat), 395 mg cholesterol, 700 mg sodium, .5 g fiber.

CHEF'S NOTES:

• This cake freezes well. I keep 2 layers in my freezer for surprise company. When they pop in, remove cake from the freezer. Top one layer with fresh homemade strawberry jam and a thick layer of ice cream. Top ice cream with a second layer of cake and then whipped cream.

• For 4 people cut a single layer in half and build the cake as described.

ROSTED COFFEE-FLAVORED LIQUEUR CREAMS

Warning: These bars are habit forming.

BARS
- 1 cup raisins
- 1 cup water
- 1/4 cup coffee-flavored liqueur
- 1 cup sugar
- 1/2 cup shortening
- 2 eggs
- 2 cups all-purpose flour
- 1 teaspoon baking soda
- 1 teaspoon cinnamon
- 1/4 teaspoon ground cloves
- 1 teaspoon vanilla
- Pinch salt

FROSTING
- 1/3 cup packed brown sugar
- 3 tablespoons butter
- 1/4 cup heavy cream, whipped
- 1 1/2 cups sifted powdered sugar
- 1 teaspoon vanilla

❶ Heat oven to 350°F. Spray 13x9-inch pan with nonstick cooking spray; lightly flour.

❷ Combine raisins, water and coffee-flavored liqueur in large pot; simmer 5 minutes. Remove from heat; cool to room temperature. Drain, reserving liquid.

❸ In large bowl, beat sugar and shortening at high speed 2 minutes. Add eggs; beat at medium speed 1 minute. Add flour, baking soda, spices, vanilla, salt and one cup of the reserved liquid; beat at medium speed 1 minute. Stir in raisins by hand.

Serve these great bars with your favorite port wine.

❹ Pour batter into prepared pan. Bake 25 to 30 minutes or until golden brown. Cool completely on wire rack before frosting.

❺ To prepare Frosting, combine brown sugar, butter and cream in large pot; bring to a boil. Boil slowly 1 minute; remove from heat. Stir in powdered sugar and vanilla immediately; stir until smooth. Top bars with frosting.

2 dozen bars.

Preparation time: 25 minutes. Ready to serve: 2 hours.

Per bar: 200 calories, 7 g total fat (3 g saturated fat), 25 mg cholesterol, 85 mg sodium, 1 g fiber.

HONEY-WHOLE WHEAT BREAD

A wonderful bread I have to share.

4$^1/_2$	teaspoons active dry yeast
5	cups warm water (105°F to 115°F)
$^3/_4$	cup butter
$^1/_4$	cup honey
4	cups whole-wheat flour
$^1/_2$	cup sugar
$^1/_2$	cup instant potatoes
$^1/_2$	cup nonfat dry milk
1	tablespoon salt
6$^1/_4$ to 7	cups all-purpose flour

❶ Sprinkle yeast in $^1/_2$ cup of the warm water; stir to dissolve. In large bowl, combine butter, honey and remaining 4$^1/_2$ cups warm water. Stir until butter is melted.

❷ In another large bowl, combine whole-wheat flour, sugar, potatoes, dry milk and salt; mix well. Combine honey and flour mixtures; stir until smooth. Add yeast and blend. Add all-purpose flour, one cup at a time, mixing well into dough. Transfer dough to lightly floured pastry cloth; let stand 5 minutes. Knead until smooth, elastic and small bubbles appear, about 10 minutes.

❸ Place dough in greased large bowl, turning dough over to grease top. Cover with kitchen towel and let rise in warm area about 1 to 1$^1/_2$ hours or until doubled in size. Punch down dough; place on clean cutting board and divide into thirds. Cover with kitchen towel and let rest 5 minutes. Shape dough into 3 loaves; place in 3 (9x5x3-inch) greased loaf pans. Cover with kitchen towel and let rise about 1 hour or until doubled again.

❹ Heat oven to 375°F. Bake 50 to 55 minutes or until loaves are golden brown. Remove from pans; cool on wire racks away from drafts.

3 (16-slice) loaves.

Preparation time: 30 minutes.
Ready to serve: 3 hours, 15 minutes.

Per slice: 130 calories, 2 g total fat (1 g saturated fat), 4 mg cholesterol, 165 mg sodium, 2 g fiber.

CHEF'S NOTES:

• To make rolls, shape dough into balls the size of golf balls. Bake the same as for loaves.

• Additional all-purpose flour may be needed because absorption differs from batch to batch.

BREAD PUDDING

*I don't know if I've ever met anyone that doesn't like bread pudding —
warm, sweet, satisfying. Here's how I make it.*

PUDDING
- 6 eggs
- 3 egg yolks
- 3/4 cup packed brown sugar
- 1 quart half-and-half
- 2 teaspoons vanilla
- 1/2 cup melted butter
- 1/2 teaspoon nutmeg
- 1/4 teaspoon cinnamon
- 6 cups cubed sweet rolls (1 1/2 inches)
- 1/2 cup raisins

SAUCE
- 1 lb. packed brown sugar
- 3/4 cup water
- 2/3 cup corn syrup
- 1/2 cup butter
- 1 tablespoon vanilla
- 2 cups heavy cream, whipped
- 1/2 cup orange-flavored liqueur

❶ Heat oven to 375°F.

❷ In large bowl, beat eggs and yolks at medium speed until frothy.

❸ In another large bowl, cream brown sugar, half-and-half, vanilla, butter, nutmeg and cinnamon; blend well with wire whisk. Add cubed sweet rolls and raisins; let stand 15 minutes. Gently mix, being careful not to break up bread cubes. Pour into 8-inch round cake pan. Place 8-inch round cake pan into 9-inch round cake pan. Place pans in oven, filling 9-inch pan as full as possible with hot water.

❹ Using another 8-inch round cake pan, trace bottom of pan along parchment paper; butter 8-inch round parchment. Cover pudding with buttered parchment; bake 1 1/2 hours or until knife inserted near center comes out clean. Serve hot with sauce.

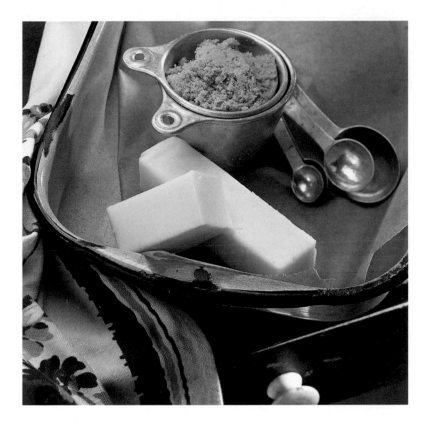

❺ To prepare Sauce, place brown sugar, water and corn syrup in medium saucepan; bring to a fast boil until candy thermometer reaches 320°F, about 10 minutes. Reduce heat to low; add butter, vanilla and orange-flavored liqueur, stirring well with wooden spoon. Remove from heat. Add cream, stirring until smooth with wooden spoon. Serve hot over pudding.

16 servings.

Preparation time: 25 minutes.

Ready to serve: 1 hour, 30 minutes.

Per serving: 400 calories, 24.5 g total fat (13.5 g saturated fat), 180 mg cholesterol, 160 mg sodium, .5 g fiber.

CHEF'S NOTES:

• For bread cubes, beforehand save and freeze leftover doughnuts, sweet rolls, caramel rolls and Danish rolls. The more caramel and filling they have, the better the flavor.

• The liqueur sauce keeps well if refrigerated. Heat in a small pot when needed. It is important to have and use a candy thermometer. It takes a long time for the sauce to reach 320°F!

• The sauce is also wonderful over ice cream or freshly-cut apple wedges.

SWEDISH RAISIN-RYE BREAD

My grandmother, Florence Hoglund Schumacher, was famous for this rye bread recipe. Her greatest delight was to trick me into eating head cheese sandwiches made with this great bread!

1/4	cup packed brown sugar
1/4	cup dark molasses
1	cup raisins
1	tablespoon salt
2	tablespoons butter
1 1/2	cups boiling water
2 1/4	teaspoons dry yeast
1/4	cup warm water
2 1/2	cups rye flour
3 to 3 1/2	cups all-purpose flour

❶ In large bowl, combine brown sugar, molasses, raisins, salt, butter and 1 1/2 cups boiling water; stir until sugar is dissolved and butter is melted. Cool to lukewarm.

❷ Sprinkle yeast in warm water, stirring to dissolve. Stir rye flour into brown sugar mixture, beat at medium speed until smooth. Stir in yeast; beat at medium speed until smooth. Gradually, mix in all-purpose flour, first with a large spoon and then by hand to make smooth, soft dough. Place dough on lightly floured pastry cloth; let rest five minutes. Knead until smooth, elastic and small bubbles appear, about 10 minutes.

❸ Place dough in greased large bowl, turning dough over to grease top. Cover and let rise in warm area about 1 to 1 1/2 hours or until doubled in size. Punch down dough; place on lightly floured pastry cloth and divide in half. Cover with kitchen towel and let rest 10 minutes. Shape dough into 2 loaves; place in 2 (9x5x3-inch) loaf pans. Cover with kitchen towel and let rise about 1 1/2 to 2 hours or until doubled again.

❹ Heat oven to 375°F. Bake loaves 25 to 30 minutes or until loaves are golden brown. Remove from pans; cool on wire racks away from drafts. Brush tops with butter.

2 (16-slice) loaves.

Preparation time: 50 minutes.
Ready to serve: 4 hours, 30 minutes.

Per slice: 90 calories, 1 g fat (.5 g saturated fat), 2 mg cholesterol, 230 mg sodium, 1.5 fiber.

CHEF'S NOTES:

• You can make a delicious variation of this bread by omitting the raisins and substituting 1 1/2 tablespoons grated orange peel and 2 teaspoons grated lemon peel.

HOMEMADE ENGLISH MUFFIN SQUARES

These muffin squares are great fun to prepare with kids. Remember to be gentle when handling the risen dough squares and placing them on the hot pan.

1/4	cup butter
1 1/4	teaspoons salt
2	tablespoons sugar
1	cup half-and-half
1/4	cup cold water
1	(1/4-oz.) pkg. active dry yeast
1	egg
1	egg yolk
7 1/4	cups all-purpose flour, sifted
1/4	cup yellow cornmeal

❶ In large pot, heat butter, salt, sugar and half-and-half just to a slow boil. Immediately remove from heat; add cold water. Cool to warm (105°F to 115°F).

❷ Add yeast to butter mixture; stir to combine. Let stand 3 minutes. Beat in egg and egg yolk at medium speed. Add 7 cups of the flour; stir well to blend. Place remaining 1/4 cup flour on pastry cloth. Turn out soft dough on top of flour. Knead 50 to 75 times or until firm and elastic. Place in large greased bowl. Cover with kitchen towel; let rest about 1 hour.

> **CHEF'S NOTES:**
> • For round muffins, cut with large round cookie cutter.

❸ On pastry cloth, roll out dough to 1/4 to 1/3 inch thick. Cut into 4-inch squares; gently separate. Cover with kitchen towel and let rest about 1 hour. Dust with flour; lightly sprinkle cornmeal over top.

❹ Heat electric skillet or griddle to 375°F. Sprinkle layer of corn meal on griddle with wide metal spatula. Remove square of dough from cloth; gently place on griddle, cooking about 5 minutes on each side. Cool on wire rack or clean kitchen towel.

20 muffin squares.

Preparation time: 30 minutes.
Ready to serve: 3 hours.

Per square: 735 calories, 22.5 g total fat (12.5 g saturated fat), 160 mg cholesterol, 860 mg sodium, 4 g fiber.

COMPANY

Oh, company! The adults would play cards. The kids would run around the house or yard renewing old friendships, forging new ones, maybe sizing up a seldom-seen cousin again. What a grand time. Maybe the company was invited. Maybe they just dropped by. No matter. They were fed well, and often, with recipes the likes of these. Use them for your own company, or treat your family.

Honey-Glazed Baked Ham, page 114

CHICKEN BREAST PIZZA

Here's a different kind of pizza for you — something with real, fresh flavor... and no crust! It's great!

4   (6-oz.) boneless skinless chicken breasts
1   teaspoon garlic salt
1   teaspoon freshly ground pepper
1   cup all-purpose flour
2   tablespoons olive oil
2   large red onions, cut into 1/2-inch slices
2   large zucchinis, cut into 4x1/2-inch slices
4   large fresh mushrooms, cut into 1/4-inch slices
2   cups pizza sauce
2   tomatoes, cut into 1/4-inch slices
1   teaspoon dried oregano
2   teaspoons chopped fresh basil
1   cup shredded mozzarella cheese

❶ Heat oven to 375°F. Spray 15x10x1-inch pan with nonstick cooking spray. Place chicken breasts, one at a time, in resealable plastic bag. Flatten with meat mallet to about 1/4 inch thickness. Season with garlic salt and pepper. Dredge in flour; shaking off excess.

❷ In large skillet, heat 1 tablespoon of the oil over medium heat until hot. Add onion slices; cook until tender. Transfer onions to serving plate. Add zucchinis and mushrooms to skillet; cook until almost tender but still crisp. Remove from pan. Add remaining 1 tablespoon oil. Sauté both sides of chicken breasts until light golden brown and no longer pink in center; transfer to pan.

❸ Place 1 tablespoon pizza sauce, 1 onion slice, 2 slices tomato, 2 zucchini strips and mushroom slices on each chicken breast. Top with 2 tablespoons pizza sauce; sprinkle with spices and generous amount of mozzarella cheese.

❹ Bake 20 minutes and serve.

4 servings.

Preparation time: 40 minutes.
Ready to serve: 1 hour.

Per serving: 615 calories, 25 g total fat (8 g saturated fat), 125 mg cholesterol, 1110 mg sodium, 7 g fiber.

CHEF'S NOTES:
• Pheasant breasts may be used in place of chicken breasts.

USHROOMS KATHLEEN

This is the most popular appetizer at our restaurant.

12 large mushroom caps
 1 lb. butter, softened
¼ cup cooked crumbled bacon
¼ cup minced shallots
 1 tablespoon chopped fresh parsley
 2 tablespoons garlic powder
12 large sea scallops

❶ Heat oven to 350°F.

❷ Wash and dry mushrooms. Place mushrooms, hollow side up in 3-quart casserole. In medium bowl, combine butter, bacon, shallots, parsley and garlic; stir well. Place 1 teaspoon garlic-butter in each mushroom cap; top with 1 scallop. Cover each cap with 1 rounded teaspoon garlic-butter mixture.

❸ Bake until golden brown and scallops turn opaque, about 20 minutes. Serve with toast points, if desired.

4 servings.

Preparation time: 20 minutes. Ready to serve: 40 minutes.

Per serving: 270 calories, 23.5 g total fat (14 g saturated fat), 75 mg cholesterol, 280 mg sodium, 1 g fiber.

> **CHEF'S NOTES:**
> • Pine nuts can be substituted for bacon.
>
> • For a more complex taste, add 1 escargot per mushroom cap.
>
> • For fish-stuffed mushrooms, use 1-inch skinless boneless fish cubes. Cook until fish flakes easily with fork.

SCALOPPINI

The best meat to use is from the loin or the tenderloins themselves. Turkey tenderloins may also be used.

8 (3-oz.) slices veal or pork
1/2 cup prepared *Seasoned Flour* (page 9)
2 teaspoons minced fresh parsley
1 teaspoon grated lemon peel
1/2 teaspoon freshly ground pepper
2 tablespoons prepared *Clarified Butter* (page 9)
2 tablespoons finely diced shallots
1 garlic clove, finely minced
1/2 cup dry white wine
2 teaspoons minced fresh tarragon

❶ Dredge veal slices in flour; shaking off excess. Set aside.

❷ In large bowl, combine parsley, lemon peel and pepper.

❸ In large skillet, melt butter over medium heat; add shallots and garlic. Top with veal slices. sauté veal until browned, about 2 minutes. Turn, stir shallots and brown opposite side; add wine and tarragon. Simmer 2 minutes.

❹ Transfer veal to heated serving platter. Sprinkle with parsley mixture. Top with sauce from pan. Serve with pasta, egg noodles or spätzles, if desired.

4 servings.

Preparation time: 10 minutes.
Ready to serve: 25 minutes.

Per serving: 175 calories, 6 g total fat (3.5 g saturated fat), 70 mg cholesterol, 450 mg sodium, 1 g fiber.

CHEF'S NOTES:

• This is excellent prepared with chicken breast. Remove skin from chicken breast and flatten with a meat mallet to 1/4 inch thick.

BEER-CHEESE SOUP

Beer-Cheese Soup curdles easily. Prepare as close to serving time as possible. If soup does curdle, blend well on medium speed.

- 1 tablespoon butter
- 1 cup peeled cubed celery (1/4 inch)
- 1/2 cup cubed white onions (1/4 inch)
- 2 garlic cloves, finely minced
- 1 tablespoon all-purpose flour
- 1 quart prepared *Chicken Stock* (page 8)
- 1 1/2 cups beer (room temperature)
- 1 1/2 cups prepared *Roux* (page 10)
- 2 lb. grated sharp cheddar cheese
- 1/2 teaspoon white pepper
- 3 drops red pepper sauce
- 1 teaspoon Worcestershire sauce
- 2 cups half-and-half
- 1 teaspoon chopped chives
- 2 cups popped popcorn

❶ In large skillet, melt butter over medium heat. Add celery and onions; cook until celery is just tender, about 2 minutes. Add garlic and flour; stir until combined.

❷ Add Chicken Stock and beer; simmer over medium heat 5 minutes. Whisk in Roux to make smooth, lump-free base. Simmer 10 minutes, stirring frequently to prevent burning. Reduce heat to low; stir in cheese, pepper, red pepper sauce and Worcestershire sauce.

❸ Pour half-and-half into medium bowl. Ladle hot cheese mixture slowly into bowl to warm half-and-half. When mixture is hot; add slowly to soup, stirring constantly with wooden spoon. Return to a simmer. Do not boil.

❹ Serve sprinkled with chives and popcorn.

6 servings.

Preparation time: 10 minutes.
Ready to serve: 35 minutes.

Per serving: 1020 calories, 79.5 g total fat (50 g saturated fat), 235 mg cholesterol, 1800 mg sodium, 1 g fiber.

CHEF'S NOTES:

- For an extra zing, add pepper cheese (use half cheddar, half pepper cheese).
- For extra-rich soup, use light cream instead of half-and-half.
- Stir often to keep from scorching.

$\mathcal{V}$EAL OR PORK SHANK

Fresh boiled potatoes and Potato Dumplings *(page 23) make excellent accompaniments for this recipe.*

8 medium fresh pork hocks
1 quart water
1 teaspoon salt
2 bay leaves
4 cups prepared *Schumacher Hotel Sauerkraut* (page 27)

❶ Remove excess fat and silver skin from meat. In large pot, heat pork hocks, water, salt and bay leaves to a boil 30 minutes. Transfer pork hocks to 3-quart casserole.

❷ Heat oven to 350°F. Pour Schumacher Hotel Sauerkraut over pork hocks. Cover and bake until meat is tender, about 1½ hours.

4 servings.
Preparation time. 15 minutes.
Ready to serve: 3 hours, 15 minutes.

Per serving: 345 calories, 11 g total fat (4 g saturated fat), 85 mg cholesterol, 2192 mg sodium, 7.5 g fiber.

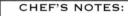

CHEF'S NOTES:

• You can also use veal. Use 4 veal shanks, as they are much larger than pork.

• You can also use smoked pork hocks for this dish.

Serve with honey wheat bread and honey.

QUICK AND EASY STIR FRY

This stir fry works well with all game and fowl meat — almost anything!
I also toss in some shrimp, just for fun. Serve with white rice or wild rice.
This is a great dish to do over a hot campfire in a heavy black skillet.

- 1 lb. beef
- 1 tablespoon cornstarch
- ½ cup prepared *Beef Stock* (page 8)
- 1 tablespoon vegetable oil
- 2 onions, sliced (¼ inch)
- 2 ribs celery, peeled, sliced (¼ inch)
- 2 carrots, cut diagonally sliced (¼ inch)
- 1 cup fresh or frozen (thawed) snow pea pods
- 4 green onions, sliced (¼ inch)
- 1 tablespoon diced fresh ginger (¼ inch)
- ¼ cup soy sauce

❶ Remove all bones, fat and silver skin from meat. Cut into 3x½-inch pieces.

❷ In large bowl, combine cornstarch with Beef Stock.

❸ In large skillet, heat oil over medium heat until hot. Brown meat on all sides. Transfer meat to clean bowl; reserving oil. Set aside.

❹ Add onions, celery and carrots to skillet; sauté until onions and celery are transparent. Add pea pods, green onions, ginger, soy sauce and browned meat; simmer 2 minutes. Stir in cornstarch mixture; mix well. Simmer on medium heat until slightly thickened.

❺ Serve with white or wild rice, if desired.

4 servings.

Preparation time: 20 minutes.
Ready to serve: 30 minutes.

Per serving: 230 calories, 7 g total fat (2 g saturated fat), 60 mg cholesterol, 1120 mg sodium, 3 g fiber.

CHEF'S NOTES:

• If using chicken or fowl, replace beef stock with Chicken Stock.

• Any vegetables will work if you don't have snow pea pods.

• I keep gingerroot frozen for this recipe. Simply remove skin with a spoon while root is frozen, then dice into small pieces.

• This also hits the spot over baked potatoes.

PHEASANT A LA CREME

This is a recipe I grew up with. My mother still makes the best in the universe.

  2 (3- to 3½-lb.) pheasants, quartered
1½ cups prepared *Seasoned Flour* (page 9)
  1 cup vegetable oil
¼ cup minced shallots
  3 cups prepared *Chicken Stock* (page 8)
  4 cups heavy cream, whipped
  2 cups sliced mushrooms (¼ inch)
1½ teaspoon salt
  6 tablespoons cream sherry
  6 tablespoons white wine

❶ Heat oven to 350°F.

❷ Roll pheasant in flour; shaking off excess. In large skillet, heat oil over medium heat until hot; brown pheasant in oil.

❸ Transfer pheasant to Dutch oven; add minced shallots and Chicken Stock. Bring to a boil. Cover and bake 2 hours. Add cream, mushrooms, salt, sherry and wine; bake an additional 1½ hours or until pheasant is tender and sauce is thick. Season with salt and pepper.

4 servings.

Preparation time: 30 minutes. Ready to serve: 4 hours.

Per serving: 1485 calories, 88 g total fat (38 g saturated fat), 475 mg cholesterol, 2955 mg sodium, 1.5 g fiber.

> **CHEF'S NOTES:**
>
> • The secret to preparing moist, tender pheasant is to cook it, covered in Chicken Stock, over moderate heat for a long period of time.
>
> • Rabbit can also be prepared this way.
>
> • You must use the heaviest cream available to get the sauce to thicken. Do not substitute milk for cream, as milk will not thicken; milk will make a curdled mess.

Serve with roasted figs, apples and plums.

STUFFED STEAKS WITH GREEN CHILE POCKETS

An interesting way to create something new and different with steak.

STEAK
 4 (10-oz.) steaks (1 inch thick)

RUB
 1 tablespoon freshly ground pepper
 1 tablespoon Cajun seasoning
 1/2 teaspoon garlic powder
 2 teaspoons olive oil

STUFFING
 2 tablespoons olive oil
 2 onions, diced (1/4 inch)
 2 (4-oz.) cans green chiles
 1 teaspoon dry oregano
 1 teaspoon chopped fresh basil
 3/4 cup prepared *Fresh Bread Crumbs* (page 31)

❶ Remove all excess fat and silver from skin. Cut deep horizontal pocket into each steak, leaving 1/2 inch on sides and end.

❷ To prepare Rub, combine pepper, Cajun seasoning and garlic powder in medium bowl; mix well. Rub on steak. Refrigerate steak in resealable plastic bag with olive oil overnight.

❸ To make Stuffing, heat oil in medium skillet over high heat until hot. Add onions and sauté until tender; add chiles and spices. Simmer 5 minutes over low heat. Add Fresh Bread Crumbs; combine well to make thick vegetable paste.

❹ Heat grill. Stuff steaks with 2 tablespoons chile stuffing. Spray outside of steak with olive oil cooking spray. Place steaks on gas grill over medium heat or on charcoal grill 4 to 6 inches from medium coals until steaks are of desired doneness.

4 servings.

Preparation time: 20 minutes. Ready to serve: 24 hours.

Per serving: 460 calories, 18 g total fat (4 g saturated fat), 150 mg cholesterol, 400 mg sodium, 3 g fiber.

> **CHEF'S NOTES:**
> • If you like it hot, add hot peppers of your choice.

HONEY-GLAZED BAKED HAM

This is the best way I know to make a ham for company.

HONEY GLAZE

1	cup dill pickle juice
1	cup packed brown sugar
1	tablespoon yellow mustard
1/2	teaspoon ground cloves
1/4	teaspoon cinnamon
1/2	cup honey
1	cup pineapple juice
1/2	cup chopped onions
1/4	teaspoon cayenne pepper
1/4	cup cornstarch

HAM

1	(4.5 lb.) shank half ham, bone-in

❶ In blender, combine pickle juice, brown sugar, mustard, cloves, cinnamon, honey, pineapple juice, onions, cayenne pepper and cornstarch; process until smooth. Pour mixture into large pot; bring to a slow boil. Simmer 5 minutes on low heat, stirring constantly.

❷ Heat oven to 300°F. Remove excess fat and skin from ham. Place ham on baking rack in roasting pan. Score ham on all sides. For appearance, press whole clove into each scored square.

❸ Bake uncovered 2 hours. With pastry brush, baste top of ham with light coating of honey glaze. Repeat every 10 to 15 minutes up to 1 hour or until internal temperature reaches 175°F.

❹ Transfer ham to serving platter. Brush with last thick layer of glaze. Reheat remaining glaze to boiling; serve as sauce. Slice ham and serve with hot glaze in sauce boat.

8 servings.

Preparation time: 15 minutes.
Ready to serve: 4 hours, 15 minutes.

Per serving: 540 calories, 17 g total fat (6 g saturated fat), 115 mg cholesterol, 3060 mg sodium, .5 g fiber.

CHEF'S NOTES:

• The glaze will not permeate the meat, but it does give the meat a great appearance and tasty outer crust. This glaze may also be used with chicken or pork chops.

• Remove whole cloves before serving.

• A boneless turkey breast is excellent roasted this way.

$\mathscr{T}$HE WORLD'S BEST FRUIT SALAD

My mother always made this for company. There were never leftovers, nor are there now. If by some miracle there are some leftovers, store tightly covered in the refrigerator for no more than 24 hours.

      2 cups peeled cubed apples (¹/₂ inch)
      1 cup peeled cubed pears (¹/₂ inch)
      2 cups cold water
      2 teaspoons lemon juice
      2 tablespoons powdered sugar
    ¹/₂ teaspoon cinnamon
      2 cups extra-heavy cream, whipped
      1 teaspoon vanilla
      1 cup sliced fresh strawberries (¹/₄ inch)
      1 cup cubed banana (¹/₂ inch)

❶ In large bowl, combine apple and pear cubes in water with lemon juice. Set aside.

❷ In small bowl, sift together powdered sugar and cinnamon; chill 30 minutes. Add cream and vanilla to sugar mixture.

❸ Drain diced apples and pears; pat dry. Place in chilled bowl. Add strawberries and bananas. Top with whipped cream and gently fold together. Serve immediately.

4 servings.

Preparation time: 20 minutes.
Ready to serve: 20 minutes.

Per serving: 540 calories, 45 g total fat (27.5 g saturated fat), 165 mg cholesterol, 45 mg sodium, 4 g fiber.

CHEF'S NOTES:

• Add or substitute your favorite fruit. Make sure all fruits are firm with no extra liquid.

• Do not cheat. Use extra-heavy cream. Remember, you deserve it!

FAMILY PICNICS

Memorial Day, the Fourth of July, Labor Day — these were the three big picnic days of the year, along with family reunions. Whatever the occasion, the food was unbelievably good. Everyone would gather at the city park, or maybe a lake resort, and unveil recipes the likes of what follows. I hope you enjoy them too, at your own special memory-making occasions.

Homemade Vanilla Custard Ice Cream, page 121

117

 OUNTY BEANS

I got this recipe when I was in the Navy, cooking for the crew on a submarine. My leading commissary man, Soupy Campbell, was kind enough to share it.

1	(15-oz.) can kidney beans, drained
1	(15.5-oz.) can butter beans, drained
2	(15-oz.) cans pork and beans
1	cup packed brown sugar
1¼	cups sliced onions (¼ inch)
½	cup ketchup
2	teaspoons mustard
⅓	cup dill pickle juice
¼	cup maple syrup

❶ In large pot, combine beans, sugar, onions, ketchup, mustard, pickle juice and syrup; stir gently. Bring to a boil over medium heat. Reduce heat; simmer, uncovered over low heat, 45 minutes or until onions are tender.

4 servings.

Preparation time: 10 minutes.
Ready to serve: 1 hour.

Per serving: 625 calories, 3 g total fat (1 g saturated fat), 15 g cholesterol, 1875 mg sodium, 17.5 g fiber.

CHEF'S NOTES:

• These beans are great hot or cold. They are a must with fried fish and potatoes.

• For added flavor, brown 1 lb. ground pork or beef and add it during the last 15 minutes of simmering.

• Do not omit the pickle juice, as it gives this dish its special flavor.

CAMPFIRE CHICKEN STEW WITH DUMPLINGS

This is a great camp recipe. If you are using it for camping, you must set yourself up well at home by precutting the vegetables. Store vegetables and dry ingredients in resealable plastic bags.

1/3	cup olive oil
2	chickens, halved, each cut into 6 pieces
4	ribs celery, cut into 1-inch pieces
4	onions, cut into 1-inch cubes
4	carrots, sliced (1/4 inch)
1/3	cup all-purpose flour
5	cups water
1/4	cup chicken base
6	potatoes, cut into 1-inch cubes
2	cups frozen peas, thawed
2	cups halved mushrooms
1	teaspoon dried thyme
1/2	teaspoon freshly ground pepper
10	prepared *Baking Powder Dumplings* (page 18)

❶ In Dutch oven, heat oil until hot. Add chicken, 4 pieces at a time until just brown, about 6 to 8 minutes. Add celery, onions and carrots; cook until onions are transparent and just tender. Add one-half the flour; stir well with wooden spoon. Add water and chicken base; stir to combine, about 4 minutes.

❷ In large bowl, combine potatoes, peas, mushrooms, remaining flour, thyme and pepper. Add to stew and mix gently. Cook 20 minutes.

❸ Prepare Baking Powder Dumplings. Place in stew; cover and cook until dumplings are tender and chicken is no longer pink in center, about 10 minutes.

8 servings.

Preparation time: 20 minutes.
Ready to serve: 1 hour, 18 minutes.

Per serving: 740 calories, 35 g total fat (8 g saturated fat), 180 mg cholesterol, 475 mg sodium, 7 g fiber.

CHEF'S NOTES:
• You can use 5 cups of Chicken Stock (page 8) if desired, instead of water.

CHICKEN FOR THE BARBECUE

Great barbecue chicken is a real treat. Here's how I do it.

- 2 chickens, cut into 8 pieces
- 1½ quarts water
- 2 bottles barbecue sauce
- 2 bay leaves
- 1 cup diced onions (½ inch)
- 2 tablespoons chicken soup base

❶ In large pot, combine chicken, water, barbecue sauce, bay leaves, onions and chicken base. Bring to a slow boil; simmer 30 minutes or until chicken is almost tender. Remove from liquid. Cook on barbecue grill or pan-broil with your favorite barbecue sauce until chicken is no longer pink in center. Brown and serve.

16 pieces.

Preparation time: 10 minutes.
Ready to serve: 1 hour, 15 minutes.

Per piece: 370 calories, 18.5 g total fat (5 g saturated fat), 130 mg cholesterol, 400 mg sodium, .5 g fiber.

CHEF'S NOTES:

• This is the best way to do barbecue chicken and it will keep the chicken moist and ensure it is done all the way through.

• This recipe also works well on game hens.

HOMEMADE VANILLA CUSTARD ICE CREAM

This is a treasured family recipe from our farm in Wheaton, Minnesota. There is absolutely nothing like homemade ice cream.

2 tablespoons unflavored gelatin
3 cups milk
2 cups sugar
1/4 teaspoon salt
5 teaspoons vanilla
6 pasteurized eggs
1½ quarts heavy cream, whipped (6 cups)
1 (3/4-oz.) box vanilla instant pudding mix

❶ In large bowl, sprinkle gelatin over 1/2 cup of the cold milk; let stand 5 minutes. In small saucepan, heat 1½ cups milk to a simmer; stir into gelatin mixture until dissolved. Stir in sugar, salt, vanilla and remaining 1 cup milk.

❷ In another large bowl, beat eggs at high speed 5 minutes. Add gelatin mixture, cream and pudding mix. Beat well; place in metal container of ice cream freezer. Place container in freezer bucket and pack with ice and kosher (coarse) salt. (Ice and salt should be layered: 3 inches of ice and 1/2 cup salt until layers come to top of mixer.)

❸ Mix ice cream. If using electric ice cream freezer, when ice cream is ready, freezer will pull harder and stop. If mixing by hand, crank will become almost impossible to move.

❹ When ice cream is frozen and stiff, remove from outer bucket and serve. (If you prefer ice cream to be firmer, place container in freezer compartment of refrigerator 1 hour.)

1 gallon.
Preparation time: 15 minutes. Ready to serve: 1 hour.

Per cup: 220 calories, 15.25 g total fat (9.25 g saturated fat), 90 mg cholesterol, 105 mg sodium, 0 g fiber.

> **CHEF'S NOTES:**
> • I recommend using pure vanilla. It has a far superior flavor.
> • For fruit-flavored ice cream, add 1½ cups mashed fresh fruit of your choice. Add when ice cream just starts to freeze and becomes difficult to mix.
> • When packing the ice cream freezer, it is important to layer ice and salt as described above. Otherwise, it will take much longer for ice cream to freeze.

KABOBS

*Use any red meat or game for these kabobs. Use any vegetables you like;
what I list here are just suggestions. Whatever you use, remember to precook
them first.*

16 (2-inch) cubes meat of choice
 2 cups vinegar and oil dressing
 8 jumbo fresh mushrooms, stems removed
 1 cup sherry
 8 pearl onions or shallots, peeled, blanched in 1-quart salted water
 8 (2-inch) pieces red or green bell peppers, blanched in 1-quart
     salted water
 8 slices fresh pineapple (1/2 inch thick)
 8 slices zucchini (1/2 inch thick)
 4 (12-inch) bamboo or metal skewers

❶ In large bowl, cover meat with herb dressing; refrigerate 24 hours.

❷ In medium pot, simmer mushrooms in sherry until tender; drain,
reserving liquid.

❸ Place meat and vegetables on skewers in this order: mushroom, onion,
meat, bell pepper, zucchini, meat, pineapple, meat, zucchini, bell pepper,
meat, onion and mushroom.

❹ Heat grill. Place skewers on gas grill over medium heat or on charcoal
grill 4 to 6 inches from medium coals. Grill until meat and vegetables are
done to your liking. While grilling, baste with liquid from mushrooms.

4 servings.

Preparation time: 30 minutes.
Ready to serve: 24 hours, 15 minutes.

Per serving: 1295 calories, 52 g total fat (12.75 g saturated fat),
465 mg cholesterol, 810 mg sodium, 2.5 g fiber.

CHEF'S NOTES:

• For fresh pineapple,
split pineapple in half and
cut pineapple chunks
from the skin with a
grapefruit knife.

BAKED SWEET POTATOES ON THE HALF SHELL

Sweet potatoes and yams work equally well in this recipe. Either way, use medium-sized potatoes.

4	medium sweet potatoes
1/3	cup cubed red onions
1	tablespoon Dijon mustard
1	teaspoon Worcestershire sauce
1/2	teaspoon salt
1/4	teaspoon freshly ground pepper
1/2	teaspoon Hungarian paprika
1	tablespoon softened butter
1	cup prepared whole-wheat *Fresh Bread Crumbs* (page 31)

❶ Heat oven to 375°F. Wash and arrange sweet potatoes on 15x10x1-inch baking pan; bake 40 minutes.

❷ Meanwhile, place onions, mustard, Worcestershire sauce, salt, pepper, paprika and butter in blender; process at medium speed until smooth. In large bowl, combine Fresh Bread Crumbs and onion mixture.

CHEF'S NOTES:

• If you wish, add 1/3 cup crumbled cooked bacon to bread crumb mixture.

• 1/3 cup chopped pecans are also a nice addition.

• To prepare this dish in advance, roast potatoes 30 minutes. Do not split. Cool and keep in the refrigerator. Before serving, cut in half and top with bread crumb mixture. Bake 40 minutes at 350°F.

❸ Slice sweet potatoes in half lengthwise. Top each half with equal amount of Fresh Bread Crumb mixture. Reduce oven temperature to 350°F. Bake an additional 30 minutes.

4 servings.

Preparation time: 10 minutes.
Ready to serve: 1 hour, 15 minutes.

Per serving: 185 calories, 4 g total fat (2 g saturated fat), 8 mg cholesterol, 450 mg sodium, 5 g fiber.

OLD FASHIONED POTATO SALAD OR MACARONI SALAD

Everyone loves potato salad, and this potato salad recipe is as easy to make as any I know.

6   russet potatoes or 6 cups cooked macaroni
1   tablespoon olive oil
2   ribs celery, peeled, diced (1/4 inch)
2   onions, diced (1/4 inch)
1   cup prepared *Basic Salad Dressing Sauce* (page 12)
4   hard-cooked eggs, peeled
2   teaspoons chopped fresh parsley

❶ In large pot, boil potatoes in salted water. Drain; let stand and cool until only slightly warm. Peel and dice into 1/2-inch cubes. Place in large bowl in refrigerator until needed.

❷ While potatoes are cooking, heat olive oil in large skillet over medium-high heat until hot. Add celery and onions; sauté 30 seconds. Remove vegetables; refrigerate.

❸ In large bowl, combine potatoes, celery, onions and Basic Salad Dressing Sauce. Cut eggs into 1/2-inch dice; add to bowl. Mix gently and let stand 1 hour. Sprinkle parsley over salad.

7 cups.

Preparation time: 30 minutes. Ready to serve: 2 hours.

Per cup: 645 calories, 44 g total fat (7 g saturated fat), 240 mg cholesterol,
625 mg sodium, 6 g fiber.

CHEF'S NOTES:

• You may add 1/4 cup diced onions or peppers if you wish. But remember: With onions this salad will not keep for long.

HAMBURGERS

Hamburgers are easy, yes. But there are many secrets to making them great, which I share in my Chef's Notes.

1½ lb. fresh or frozen (thawed) ground beef
1 teaspoon salt
½ teaspoon freshly ground pepper
¼ cup tomato juice

❶ In small bowl, combine salt, pepper and tomato juice. Pour mixture evenly over meat; mix well with hands to combine.

❷ Fill 1 (6-oz.) coffee cup or bouillon cup to the top with meat; press firmly. Turn burger mound onto clean plate; shape into patties. Keep patties refrigerated until use.

❸ Heat large skillet to medium-hot. Add patties; brown well. Turn and cook until internal temperature reaches 160°F. Remove from pan; season to taste.

❹ Or, heat grill to 375°F. Place burgers on grill over medium heat or on charcoal grill 4 to 6 inches from medium coals. Rotate to mark. When burger is well-browned, turn over with spatula or tongs. Cook until internal temperature reaches 160°F.

❺ For cheeseburger, add your favorite cheese after burger is done; cook until cheese is melted.

4 servings.

Preparation time: 5 minutes.

Ready to serve: 15 minutes.

Per servings: 355 calories, 24 g total fat (9.5 g saturated fat), 100 mg cholesterol, 715 mg sodium, .15 g fiber.

CHEF'S NOTES:

• Use the freshest of ground beef from an inspected shop.

• If you have frozen meat, thaw it in a refrigerator that is at 38°F to 40°F.

• Make sure your hands are clean. Make sure all grilling utensils are clean.

• Never, never press burgers, as this dries out the juices and flavor.

• Only turn burgers once, as each time you turn them dries out the juices.

• Never poke the burger with a fork or knife as you could contaminate the meat.

• You must cook all ground meat to at least 160°F to kill bacteria. This is very important.

• Never put salt on burgers until after they are cooked, as the salt will otherwise draw out the juices.

• Always transfer cooked burgers to a clean plate.

MARINATED CUCUMBERS

Cucumbers are a boom or bust proposition. When you're in a boom, here's what to do with some of them.

5	medium cucumbers, peeled, sliced (1/4 inch)
1	cup finely chopped green bell pepper
1/2	teaspoon grated lemon peel
2	onions, finely chopped
1	cup white vinegar
2	cups sugar
1	teaspoon celery seed
2	teaspoons salt

❶ In large bowl, combine cucumbers, bell pepper, lemon peel and onions; mix well. Set aside.

❷ In large saucepan, combine vinegar, sugar, celery seed and salt; bring to a boil immediately. Remove from heat; refrigerate, covered, at least 4 hours.

❸ Add chilled vinegar mixture to cucumber mix; toss gently. Place in 2 1/2-quart container; cover and refrigerate.

7 cups.

Preparation time: 20 minutes. Ready to serve: 4 hours.

Per cup: 160 calories, .5 g total fat (0 g saturated fat), 0 mg cholesterol, 300 mg sodium, 3.5 g fiber.

CREAMY COLESLAW DRESSING WITH HORSERADISH

Don't settle for store-bought coleslaw. Make your own batch, fresh, with this recipe.

- 3 cups mayonnaise
- 2 tablespoons sugar
- 1/2 teaspoon salt, plus more to taste
- 1/2 teaspoon freshly ground pepper, plus more to taste
- 1 tablespoon yellow mustard
- 1/3 cup half-and-half
- 1 teaspoon Worcestershire sauce
- 2 teaspoons celery seed
- 3 tablespoons lemon juice
- 1/3 cup dry horseradish
- 1 head cabbage, shredded
- 1 peeled shredded carrot

❶ In large bowl, combine mayonnaise, sugar, salt, pepper, mustard, half-and-half, Worcestershire sauce, celery seed and lemon juice; blend until smooth. Add horseradish. Store in refrigerator.

❷ In another large bowl combine cabbage and carrot. Pour dressing over slaw; mix well. Adjust seasoning to taste.

8 servings.

Preparation time: 5 minutes.
Ready to serve: 5 minutes.

Per serving: 230 calories, 22.5 g total fat (3.5 g saturated fat), 17.5 mg cholesterol, 235 mg sodium, 2 g fiber.

CHEF'S NOTES:
• The horseradish liquid tastes great in tomato juice or in Bloody Marys.
• Keep well-chilled and covered until served.

OLD WORLD CHEESECAKE

Here is my recipe for a traditional old world, classic cheesecake.

CRUST

- ⅓ cup butter
- ¼ cup sugar
- 4 drops almond extract
- 1 cup graham-cracker crumbs

FILLING

- 6 (8-oz.) pkg. cream cheese, softened
- 1 teaspoon all-purpose flour
- 1½ cups sugar
- 3 tablespoons fresh lemon juice
- 1 teaspoon vanilla
- ¼ teaspoon almond extract
- 12 large eggs

❶ Heat oven to 275°F. Lightly grease 10-inch springform pan with butter; dust with flour, shaking out excess.

❷ In large saucepan, melt butter over medium-high heat. Add sugar; stir to dissolve. Add almond and graham-cracker crumbs to butter mixture; blend well. Spread graham-cracker crust mixture evenly into bottom of prepared pan. Refrigerate while preparing filling.

❸ In mixer, beat cream cheese at medium speed until soft and creamy. In medium bowl, sift together flour and sugar. In another medium bowl, combine lemon juice, vanilla and almond. Blend both flour and lemon juice mixtures gradually into cream cheese mixture, beating at medium speed 3 minutes or until smooth.

❹ Add eggs, 3 at a time, to cream cheese mixture, beating at low speed after each addition until light and smoothly blended.

❺ Pour batter into chilled crust. Place in oven. Immediately reduce oven temperature to 250°F. Bake about 1 hour and 15 minutes or until toothpick inserted near center comes out clean. Cool in pan at room temperature on wire rack. Store in refrigerator.

20 slices.

Preparation time: 45 minutes. Ready to serve: 6 hours, 45 minutes.

Per slice: 395 calories, 30 g total fat (18 g saturated fat), 210 mg cholesterol, 285 mg sodium, .05 g fiber.

CELEBRATIONS

Around our house, your birthday lasted a week. By the time you had a family party (parents and siblings), relatives' party (aforementioned family plus aunts, uncles, grandparents, cousins and the like), and a friends' party, a week was gone and you were preparing for the next gala of bashes! Here are the recipes that made these celebrations, and others, extra-special.

Rhubarb Pie, page 138

CHERRY NUT CAKE ON YOUR BIRTHDAY

This is the cake my mom made for my birthdays.

¹/₃ cup butter, softened
¹/₃ cup vegetable shortening
1¹/₂ cups sugar
3 cups sifted cake flour
2¹/₂ teaspoons baking powder
1 teaspoon salt
¹/₄ cup maraschino cherry juice
³/₄ cup half-and-half
16 maraschino cherries, quartered
¹/₂ cup chopped walnuts
6 egg whites
White Divinity Frosting (recipe follows)

❶ Heat oven to 350°F. Grease and flour 2 (9-inch) round cake pans.

❷ In large bowl, beat butter, shortening and sugar at medium speed 2¹/₂ minutes. In small bowl, sift together flour, baking powder and salt.

❸ In another small bowl, combine cherry juice and half-and-half. Alternately add flour mixture and cherry juice to butter mixture. Stir in cherries and walnuts. In another large bowl, beat egg whites at medium speed until stiff peaks form; fold into batter with wire whisk. Pour into prepared pans.

❹ Bake 30 to 35 minutes or until toothpick inserted near center comes out clean. Cool on wire rack before frosting with White Divinity Frosting or whipped cream.

Continued on page 136

Continued from page 134

WHITE DIVINITY FROSTING

1/2 cup sugar
1/4 cup light corn syrup
 2 tablespoons water
 3 egg whites
 1 teaspoon vanilla
1/2 teaspoon almond extract

❶ To prepare frosting, heat sugar, corn syrup and water in small saucepan over medium heat. Bring to a boil, but do not stir. Heat to 242°F on candy thermometer, about 4 minutes.

❷ In large bowl, beat egg whites until stiff. Pour a thin stream of hot syrup into beaten egg whites, mixing constantly at medium speed until whites become stiff again, about 5 minutes; beat in vanilla and almond extract.

8 servings.

Preparation time: 45 minutes.
Ready to serve: 2 hours, 45 minutes.

Per serving: 670 calories, 24 g total fat (9 g saturated fat), 29 mg cholesterol, 590 mg sodium, 1.5 g fiber.

CHEF'S NOTES:

• To make cherry divinity frosting, substitute maraschino cherry juice for the water.

CORNED BEEF HOT DISH

This recipe is one of those great hot dishes served in the basement of the Lutheran Church in Wheaton, Minnesota. As my father, Cully, said, "That was a good feed!"

3   potatoes, peeled, diced (1/2 inch)
1   teaspoon salt
2   tablespoons butter
1   tablespoon flour
1   cup half-and-half
1   (12-oz.) can corned beef
1/4   cup chopped red onions (1/2 inch)
1   (10³/4-oz.) can tomato soup
1   (15-oz.) can butter beans, drained

❶ Heat oven to 350°F. Spray 3-quart casserole with nonstick cooking spray.

❷ In large pot, cover potatoes with water; add salt. Bring to a boil. Cook 5 minutes, drain.

❸ Melt butter in medium saucepan; stir in flour. Slowly stir in half-and-half, cooking until mixture thickens.

❹ In large bowl, break corned beef apart. Add onions, potatoes, half-and-half mixture, soup and butter beans; mix well. Spread mixture into prepared casserole. Bake 1 hour.

4 servings.

Preparation time: 20 minutes. Ready to serve: 1 hour, 5 minutes.

Per serving: 310 calories, 13.5 g total fat (6.5 g saturated fat), 56 mg cholesterol, 1110 mg sodium, 5 g fiber.

RHUBARB PIE

*For extra eye appeal, add a lattice top to this pie. This is always my wife,
Kathleen's, birthday treat!*

  1 recipe prepared *Pie Crust* (page 10)
  4 cups fresh rhubarb, cut into 1/2-inch-thick pieces
1 1/2 cups sugar
 1/2 cup packed brown sugar
 1/4 cup all-purpose flour
  2 eggs
  2 egg yolks
  3 tablespoons half-and-half
  1 teaspoon vanilla

❶ Heat oven to 350°F. Line 9-inch pie pan with pie crust.

❷ Arrange rhubarb pieces in bottom of pie crust.

❸ In large bowl, combine 1 1/2 cups sugar, 1/2 cup brown sugar and flour. In
another large bowl, combine eggs, egg yolks, half-and-half and vanilla.
Combine sugar and egg mixtures; whisk until smooth. Pour evenly over
rhubarb.

❹ Bake 55 to 60 minutes or until crust is golden brown and toothpick
inserted near center comes out
clean. Cool on wire rack.

6 servings.

Preparation time: 10 minutes.
Ready to serve: 1 hour.

Per serving: 475 calories, 15 g total fat (4 g
saturated fat), 145 mg cholesterol, 135 mg
sodium, 1.5 g fiber.

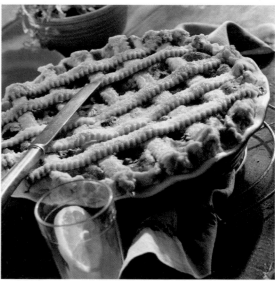

CHEF'S NOTES:

• For strawberry rhubarb
pie, use 3 cups rhubarb
pieces and 1 1/2 cups sliced
strawberry pieces.

• Do not use frozen
rhubarb as it becomes
mushy and stringy.

AMERICAN CHOP SUEY HOT DISH

This is my favorite birthday dinner, along with Cherry Nut Cake *(page 134). But this hot dish is great for any occasion! If you're not from the rural midwest, you might otherwise know "hot dish" as "casserole."*

MACARONI

3	quarts boiling water
1	tablespoon salt
2	tablespoons olive oil
1½	cups elbow macaroni

HOT DISH

1½	tablespoons olive oil
2	onions, diced (¼ inch)
2	garlic cloves, finely minced
2	lb. ground beef
2	(8-oz.) cans tomato sauce
1	(14-oz.) can diced tomatoes, undrained
1	teaspoon salt
½	teaspoon freshly ground pepper
	Dash Worcestershire sauce

❶ Heat oven to 350°F.

❷ In large pot, bring water, salt and oil to a rapid boil; add macaroni. Gently stir noodles off bottom of pan. Boil uncovered 8 minutes; drain quickly in colander. If noodles or pasta are added to sauce, rinsing is not necessary. If noodles or pasta are to be used later, rinse under cold running water 30 seconds to stop cooking.

❸ In Dutch oven, heat olive oil over medium heat until hot. Add onions and garlic; cook until onions are transparent (not brown). Break beef into egg-sized pieces; add to onions. Brown meat, stirring gently to cook thoroughly.

❹ When meat is brown, add tomato sauce, diced tomatoes and juice, salt, pepper and Worcestershire sauce. Reduce heat to low; simmer 5 minutes. Stir in cooked macaroni. Cover and bake 50 minutes to 1 hour. Serve with crisp dill pickles and hard crusted roll or bread, if desired.

8 servings.

Preparation time: 10 minutes. Ready to serve: 1 hour, 20 minutes.

Per serving: 330 calories, 17 g total fat (6 g saturated fat), 52 mg cholesterol, 655 mg sodium, 2 g fiber.

STRAWBERRIES BRANDI

This recipe is named after my daughter, Brandi, who jumped up on my lap one afternoon and said, "Daddy, why don't you name a recipe after me?" Because strawberries are Brandi's favorite fruit, I created this one for her.

- 38 extra-large strawberries, cleaned
- 1 tablespoon honey
- 1 tablespoon powdered sugar
- 1 teaspoon orange-flavored liqueur
- 2 cups heavy cream
- 32 extra-large strawberries
- 2 cups sugar

❶ Combine 6 of the strawberries, honey, powdered sugar and orange-flavored liqueur in blender; puree 30 seconds. In large bowl, beat cream at medium speed until it begins to foam and thicken. Fold in strawberry puree.

❷ Roll remaining 32 strawberries in sugar. Place 8 strawberries per serving into dessert bowl; cover with whipped cream-strawberry puree mixture. Refrigerate any leftovers.

4 servings.

Preparation time: 15 minutes. Ready to serve: 20 minutes.

Per serving: 600 calories, 38 g total fat (23 g saturated fat), 135 mg cholesterol, 45 mg sodium, 6 g fiber.

CHEF'S NOTES:

• You may also use fresh peaches instead of strawberries.

• For children, I recommend not using orange-flavored liqueur. Substitute 1 tablespoon orange juice concentrate.

HOMEMADE ONION RINGS

All vegetables work well in this recipe, as long as the pieces are small.

- 4 cups milk
- 2 teaspoons salt
- 3 dashes red pepper sauce
- 2 extra-large onions, peeled, core removed, cut into
  ¼-inch-thick rings
- 4 cups oil
- 2 cups all-purpose flour
- 1 recipe prepared *Beer-Battered Fish* (page 28)

❶ In large bowl, whisk together milk, salt and red pepper sauce. Place rings in milk mixture; toss. Let set 5 minutes; toss again.

❷ Heat oil to 375°F. Pour flour into shallow pan. Remove onion rings from milk one at a time; shaking off excess liquid. Dredge in flour, then dip in Beer-Battered Fish; shake off excess. Fry, turning once, until golden brown, about 4 to 6 minutes. Drain in paper towel-lined bowl. Keep covered until all rings are done. Season with favorite seasoning.

6 to 8 servings.

Preparation time: 15 minutes.
Ready to serving: 1 hour.

Per serving: 240 calories, 8 g total fat (1.5 g saturated fat), 3 mg cholesterol, 315 mg sodium, 2.5 g fiber.

CHEF'S NOTES:

• To make breaded rings, make 2 cups *Egg Wash* (page 9) and 4 cups *Fresh Bread Crumbs* (page 31). Place rings in milk. Roll in flour. Dip in Egg Wash and toss in Fresh Bread Crumbs. Fry until golden brown.

• For deep-fried fruit, cut fruit into ¼-inch-thick pieces no longer than 4 inches long. Fry the same as for onion rings. After frying, roll hot pieces in 1 cup granulated sugar and 1 teaspoon cinnamon mixture. Top with *Confectioners' Sugar Glaze* (page 14).

• Add seasoning after frying, while items are hot, so they can absorb the flavor.

• Grease is best heated in an electric frying pan with about 2 inches vegetable oil.

• Do not keep grease after use.

• Make sure all liquid is kept far away from hot grease.

COWBOY PIE

This will satisfy even the hungriest soul.

  1   lb. ground beef
  1   cup diced onions (1/4 inch)
1/2   cup diced red bell peppers (1/4 inch)
1 1/2   teaspoons chili powder
1/2   cup sliced fresh mushrooms (1/4 inch)
  2   cups frozen corn
  1   cup sour cream
  1   teaspoon salt
1/2   teaspoon freshly ground pepper
1/4   teaspoon red pepper sauce
  4   cooked mashed potatoes
1/4   cup butter
1/2   cup shredded cheddar cheese
  1   bunch scallions cut into 1/4-inch slices

❶ Heat oven to 375°F.

❷ In large skillet, combine ground beef, onions, bell peppers and chili powder. Cook over medium heat until meat is brown. Add mushrooms; simmer 3 minutes, stirring with wooden spoon to keep from sticking.

❸ Transfer beef mixture to 9-inch pie plate. Pour corn evenly over beef mixture. In large bowl, combine sour cream, salt, pepper and red pepper sauce. Spread evenly over corn.

❹ Spread mashed potatoes over sour cream layer. Dot with pieces of butter; top evenly with shredded cheese. Cover and bake until heated through, about 45 minutes. Garnish with chopped scallions.

4 servings.
Preparation time: 20 minutes.
Ready to serve: 1 hour, 20 minutes.

Per serving: 690 calories, 44 g total fat (23.5 g saturated fat), 150 mg cholesterol, 855 mg sodium, 5 g fiber.

CHEF'S NOTES:

• Ground pork or game, or half-pork and half-beef, are all excellent substitutes for straight ground beef.

• If you like, add a jalapeño chile (sliced) with sour cream. Remember to remove seeds and white pulp from the peppers.

• Mashed sweet potatoes or yams are a great change of flavor instead of regular potatoes.

• I also sometimes add 1/3 cup plain barbecue sauce on top of cooked meat layer.

SWEDISH MEATBALLS

For extra flavor, add 1/4 cup sherry wine with the half-and-half.

2	eggs
2 1/2	cups half-and-half
1/2	teaspoon nutmeg
1	teaspoon salt
1/4	teaspoon white pepper
2/3	cup finely minced onions
2	cups prepared *Fresh Bread Crumbs* (page 31)
1 1/2	lb. ground beef
1/2	lb. ground pork
1	cup prepared *Seasoned Flour* (page 9)
1/2	cup prepared *Clarified Butter* (page 9)
1	tablespoon all-purpose flour

❶ In large bowl, whisk together eggs, 1 cup of the half-and-half, nutmeg, salt and pepper until frothy. Add onions and Fresh Bread Crumbs; combine well.

❷ Add ground beef and ground pork. Combine mixture thoroughly with hands. Using a teaspoon, shape into tiny (1-inch) round meatballs. Roll meatballs in Seasoned Flour.

❸ In large skillet, heat Clarified Butter over medium-high heat until hot. Brown meatballs in butter until no longer pink in center. Remove meatballs from pan; keep warm.

❹ To make pan gravy, add 1 tablespoon flour to skillet. With wooden spoon, scrape up browned bits from skillet; combine with butter, stirring over low heat cook 2 minutes. Do not brown. Add remaining 1 1/2 cups half-and-half; whisk until smooth. Simmer 5 minutes. Pour over meatballs.

4 servings.

Preparation time: 15 minutes.
Ready to serve: 1 hour.

Per serving: 940 calories, 66 g total fat (32.5 g saturated fat), 330 mg cholesterol, 1480 mg sodium, 2.5 g fiber.

CHEF'S NOTES:

• I often use 1-lb. ground beef, 8-oz. ground pork and 8-oz. ground veal for the 2 total lbs. of meat.

• For a gravy shortcut, add 1 can condensed cream of mushroom or cream of celery soup to pan. Stir well with a wooden spoon over low heat. Add 2/3 cup half-and-half. Whisk and simmer 4 minutes and serve.

• Serve meatballs hot for appetizers or hors d'oeuvres. You can also serve them in a cream gravy on buttered noodles, whipped potatoes or steamed rice.

COUNTRY QUICHE

Quiche is one of those classic dishes that works for breakfast, as a lunch snack served cold, or as a light supper.

1	recipe *Pie Crust* (page 10)
¼	cup finely chopped green onions
1½	cups shredded cheddar cheese
1	cup fresh asparagus pieces (½ inch)
1	cup smoked link sausage or summer sausage sliced (⅛ inch)
1	cup cooked cubed chicken (¼ inch)
4	eggs
2	egg yolks
1½	cups half-and-half
1	teaspoon salt
¼	teaspoon freshly ground pepper

❶ Heat oven to 375°F.

❷ Prepare pie crust dough, adding chopped green onions to step 2. Roll out dough to ⅛ inch thickness. Press into 9-inch pie plate.

❸ Arrange cheese, asparagus pieces, sausage and chicken pieces in bottom of pie crust. In large bowl, whisk eggs, egg yolks, half-and-half, salt and pepper until smooth; pour over cheese mixture.

❹ Place pie plate on shallow baking sheet. Bake about 40 minutes or until toothpick inserted near center comes out clean. Let stand 10 minutes; serve with salsa.

6 servings.

Preparation time: 40 minutes.
Ready to serve: 1 hour, 30 minutes.

Per serving: 530 calories, 40.5 g total fat (17.5 g saturated fat), 310 mg cholesterol, 995 mg sodium, 1 g fiber.

CHEF'S NOTES:
• If you don't want to use fowl, use any cooked meat.

HOLIDAYS

Recipes like these, reserved for Easter, Thanksgiving, Christmas and New Year's, made the holidays special. As kids, we ate these meals in the kitchen, craning our necks and longing to be with the adults in the dining room. Once we reached the dining room, we longed to be back where it was fun and where you got to eat first — in the kitchen with the kids.

Roast Leg of Lamb, page 156

SCHUMACHER HOTEL SWEET-ROLL STUFFING

My favorite and best stuffing. Enjoy!

   Poultry giblets (see *Roast Turkey*, page 152)
4   diced onions (1/2 inch)
4   ribs celery, diced (1/2 inch)
2   bay leaves
2   quarts water
1/2   cup butter
2   garlic cloves, minced
12   oz. sausage
1   teaspoon thyme
2   teaspoons poultry seasoning
1   teaspoon sage
1   teaspoon freshly ground pepper
4   eggs
1/2   cup milk
1 1/2   tablespoons chicken base
2   cups prepared *Chicken Stock* (page 8)
12   cups dry sweet rolls, doughnuts, pastries or breads,
      cut into 1-inch cubes

❶ Heat oven to 350°F. Butter 4-quart casserole.

❷ Boil giblets with 1 cup of the onions, 1 cup of the celery, bay leaves and water. Boil until meat is tender. Strain; remove giblets. Remove meat from wings and neck. Combine with giblets. Cool and grind. Save stock.

❸ In large skillet, melt butter over medium heat. Add remaining 1 cup each onions and celery. Add garlic; sauté until onion is transparent, about 5 minutes. Add sausage, cover and cook until no longer pink in center, about 6 minutes. Set aside to cool.

Adorn your table with assorted harvest pumpkins and fruits of the season.

❹ In large bowl, blend spices, eggs, milk, chicken base, Chicken Stock and dried bread together with wire whisk. Combine all ingredients; let stand 20 minutes. Mix gently to combine, being careful not to over mix. Bake stuffing separately 2¹/₂ hours.

12 servings.

Preparation time: 1 hour. Ready to serve: 2 hours, 15 minutes.

Per serving: 330 calories, 20 g total fat (9 g saturated fat), 142 mg cholesterol, 690 mg sodium, 1.5 g fiber.

CHEF'S NOTES:

• To accumulate enough bread for this recipe, you might try cubing and freezing leftover pastries.

• When using frozen cubes, be sure to thaw them first.

• For a sweet variation on this stuffing, add ¹/₂ cup apples, ¹/₂ cup pears, ¹/₂ cup prunes — all diced large — and ¹/₂ cup raisins to the recipe. Bake and serve.

• I recommend baking stuffing separately because fowl can carry bacteria in their cavities.

GAME HENS

Game hens have a natural drama when they are served. To enhance this, top hens with a hot orange-cranberry sauce or mushroom sauce.

- 4 (1-lb.) Cornish game hens
- 4 quarts water
- 3 bay leaves
- 1½ tablespoons chicken soup base
- 2 onions, chopped (1 inch)
- ½ teaspoon freshly ground pepper
- ½ teaspoon dried thyme
- 8 teaspoons melted butter

❶ Heat oven to 350°F.

❷ Remove giblets; rinse cavities well. In large pot, combine meat, water, bay leaves, chicken base, onions, pepper, thyme and butter; cover and bring to a slow boil. Reduce heat to low; simmer 30 minutes.

❸ Remove meat from pot to 15x10x1-inch baking pan. Brush with butter. Bake 30 minutes or until no longer pink in center and juices run clear.

4 servings.

Preparation time: 10 minutes. Ready to serve: 30 minutes.

Per serving: 270 calories, 8 g total fat (2 g saturated fat), 210 mg cholesterol, 130 mg sodium, 0 g fiber.

CHEF'S NOTES:

• This is an easy and attractive recipe for entertaining. You may poach the hens as much as one day in advance, and then finish them in the oven as close to serving time as needed.

• Strain the stock and save for soup or gravy.

• Serve the hens on a mound of homemade stuffing or rice.

ROAST GOOSE

Goose is always an elegant dish for special occasions. This is our famous Christmas goose recipe served from Thanksgiving through New Year's Day at the hotel.

1   (8- to 9-lb.) goose
1   teaspoon salt
1/2 teaspoon freshly ground pepper
1   tablespoon caraway seeds
1   quart water

❶ Heat oven to 350°F.

❷ Remove giblets; reserve liver, heart, gizzard and neck. Remove wings at elbow joint. Rinse cavity well. Season with salt, pepper and caraway seeds. Place in roaster on top of wings and neck bone with 1 quart water, breast side up.

❸ Cover and bake 3½ hours.

❹ When goose is tender, drain off water and fat. Return to oven, uncovered, 10 minutes to dry and crisp skin.

4 (4-oz.) servings.

Preparation time: 15 minutes
Ready to serve: 3 to 4 hours

Per serving: 270 calories, 14.5 g total fat (5 g saturated fat), 110 mg cholesterol, 275 mg sodium, 0 g fiber.

> **CHEF'S NOTES:**
> • When you serve this, place one leg and one thigh on plate, or a half breast and wing.
>
> • By cooking domestic geese in this manner, they will stay moist and tender. Don't be hesitant to add all recommended liquid. This is a moist cooking recipe.

ROAST TURKEY

The best way I know to roast a turkey.

1   (18- to -22 lb.) turkey
2   teaspoons salt
1   teaspoon freshly ground pepper
1   cup dry white wine

❶ Heat oven to 275°F.

❷ Rinse turkey and pat dry; season with salt and pepper. Place bird in roaster bag; add wine.

❸ Bake 2¹/₂ to 3 hours or until internal temperature reaches 180°F in thickest part of breast.

20 servings.

Preparation time: 20 minutes. Ready to serve: 4 hours, 15 minutes.

Per serving: 215 calories, 8.5 g total fat (2 g saturated fat), 100 mg cholesterol, 285 mg sodium, 0 g fiber.

10 STEPS TO A PERFECT TURKEY

1. Thaw frozen turkey in refrigerator; remove wrapper. Heat oven to 300°F.

2. Remove neck from body cavity and giblets from neck cavity. Cut wings off at first joint.

3. Cook neck, giblets (except for liver, as it is too bitter) and wings in large roasting pan with 2 cups onions, 1 cup celery, 2 bay leaves, 1 teaspoon thyme, 1/2 teaspoon black pepper and 2 quarts cold water. Cook until meat is tender and no longer pink in center.

   - Remove meat from neck bone.

   - Save stock, and dice meat and giblets to be used in your favorite dressing recipe.

   - Never stuff your bird. Instead, cook stuffing in a covered baking dish.

4. Rinse turkey inside and out with cold water. Season cavity with salt and white pepper.

5. Place one large or two medium peeled onions in the cavity.

6. Rub skin lightly with vegetable oil.

7. Place turkey in roaster bag. Bake at 300°F.

8. Check for doneness 1/2 hour before turkey is expected to be done. Turkey is fully cooked when thigh's internal temperature is **180°F**.

9. When cooked thoroughly, let turkey stand 10 to 15 minutes before carving.

10. Remember that each bird is different because of age, sex and weight.

PANFISH AND OYSTER STEW

This is our family's traditional recipe for Christmas Eve lunch. Most any boneless, white-fleshed fish will work if you don't have crappies.

- 2 tablespoons butter
- 2 tablespoons finely diced shallots
- 3 cups crappies, cut into 1-inch pieces (about 2½-lb. fillets)
- ½ cup prepared *Seasoned Flour* (page 9)
- ¼ cup sherry
- 2 (8-oz.) cans oysters, undrained
- 2 teaspoons Worcestershire sauce
- ½ cup heavy cream
- 1 cup half-and-half
- 1 teaspoon chopped fresh parsley
- ⅛ teaspoon freshly ground pepper

❶ In large pot, melt butter over medium heat. Add shallots; sauté until tender. Dredge fish in Seasoned Flour; shaking off excess. Add fish; sauté 20 seconds per side.

❷ Add sherry, oysters and Worcestershire sauce to pot; bring liquid to a low boil. Reduce heat; simmer 2 minutes or until fish flakes easily with fork.

❸ In small bowl, combine cream and half-and-half. Add cream mixture to stew; return to a simmer.

❹ Gently ladle stew into bowls; top with parsley and pepper. Serve with oyster crackers.

6 cups.

Preparation time: 15 minutes.
Ready to serve: 30 minutes.

Per cup: 484 calories, 27 g total fat (15 g saturated fat), 205 mg cholesterol, 1010 mg sodium, .5 fiber.

CHEF'S NOTES:

• If shallots are not available, red onions will work.

• If using fresh-shucked oysters, strain liquid and reserve to add to soup. Rinse oysters in cold water to remove sand and dirt. Be very careful that oysters are fresh and from an approved location and vendor.

• It is important to combine cream mixture with the soup the way I suggested so stew doesn't curdle. The heavy cream also gives the right consistency and thickens the stew.

ROAST LEG OF LAMB

It is easier to use a boneless roast here, but the bone-in leg of lamb will have better flavor.

1	(5- to 6-lb.) leg of lamb, bone-in
4	garlic cloves
1½	cups sliced onions
1½	cups dry white wine
6	peeled halved potatoes (about 3 lb.)
1	cup peeled pearl onions
4	zucchinis, quartered
12	large mushrooms, quartered
6	carrots, peeled, cut 3 inches long, split lengthwise
2	cups peeled diced celery
1	teaspoon thyme
1	teaspoon tarragon
1	teaspoon salt
½	teaspoon freshly ground pepper

❶ Heat oven to 325°F.

❷ Remove excess fat and skin from roast. Puncture roast 2 inches deep with thin sharp knife in 8 to 10 places. Cut garlic cloves into thirds; place into punctures. Set roast on onions in baking pan. Add white wine; cover and place in oven. Bake 1 hour.

❸ Add vegetables and spices to pan. Cover and bake until internal temperature reaches 160°F. Transfer to platter.

❹ If vegetables are not tender, increase oven temperature to 375°F. Cover and bake until vegetables are tender, but not overcooked. Season with salt.

❺ Slice roast; serve with vegetables. Serve juices in sauce boat.

4 servings.

Preparation time: 40 minutes. Ready to serve: 3 hours.

Per serving: 875 calories, 26.5 g total fat (9 g saturated fat), 255 mg cholesterol, 325 mg sodium, 13 g fiber.

CANDIED YAM TORTE

Sweet potatoes work the same as yams in this recipe. For extra flavor, replace 2 cups sliced potatoes with 2 cups peeled, sliced, hard apples.

4 cups yams, peeled, cut into 1/4-inch slices
2 teaspoons lemon juice
1 recipe prepared *Pie Crust* (page 10)
1 cup packed brown sugar
1 tablespoon all-purpose flour
1/2 teaspoon nutmeg
1/2 teaspoon cinnamon
1 teaspoon vanilla
2 tablespoons butter, softened
2 cups marshmallows

❶ Heat oven to 375°F.

❷ Sprinkle yams with lemon juice.

❸ Place pie crust in 9-inch pie plate.

❹ In large bowl, combine brown sugar, flour, nutmeg, cinnamon and vanilla. Add yam slices and butter. Toss well to combine; fill pie crust gently, arranging slices so they do not hang over sides.

❺ Bake 1 hour. Top pie with even layer of marshmallows; bake an additional 20 minutes. Let cool 10 minutes. When baked, slices should be tender and marshmallows brown. Serve as side dish with dinner.

6 to 8 servings.

Preparation time: 30 minutes. Ready to serve: 2 hours.

Per serving: 675 calories, 23 g total fat (8 g saturated fat), 16 mg cholesterol, 230 mg sodium, 5 g fiber.

> **CHEF'S NOTES:**
> • If you are not a marshmallow fan, omit them.
> • This is an excellent treat served cold with leftovers.

CRANBERRY LOAF

This is a bread like you've never tasted before. The ingredients blend naturally and beautifully.

- 6 oz. cream cheese, softened
- 1 egg
- 1 tablespoon plus 1 cup sugar
- 2 tablespoons orange-flavored liqueur
- 2 cups all-purpose flour
- 1 1/2 teaspoons baking powder
- 1/2 teaspoon baking soda
- 1/2 teaspoon salt
- 3/4 cup apple juice
- 1/4 cup melted butter
- 1 egg, beaten
- 1 1/2 cups chopped fresh cranberries
- 1/2 cup chopped walnuts

❶ Heat oven to 350°F. Spray 9x5x3-inch loaf pan with nonstick cooking spray; lightly flour.

❷ In small bowl, beat cream cheese at medium speed until light and fluffy. Add egg, 1 tablespoon sugar and liqueur; blend well and set aside.

❸ In large bowl, mix together flour, 1 cup sugar, baking powder, baking soda and salt. Stir in apple juice, butter and egg. Fold in cranberries and walnuts.

❹ Spoon one-half of batter into prepared pan. Spoon cream cheese mixture evenly over batter. Top with remaining batter.

❺ Bake 65 to 75 minutes or until golden brown and toothpick inserted near center comes out clean; cool 15 minutes. Remove from pan; cool on wire rack. Store in refrigerator tightly wrapped in plastic.

1 (16-slice) loaf.

Preparation time: 15 minutes.
Ready to serve: 1 hour, 30 minutes.

Per serving: 220 calories, 10 g total fat (4.5 g saturated fat), 46 mg cholesterol, 220 mg sodium, 1 g fiber.

CHEF'S NOTES:

• For children, I recommend not using orange-flavored liqueur. Substitute 2 tablespoons orange juice concentrate.

CANDIED APPLES

This was one of our favorite family dishes to go with our Thanksgiving and Christmas dinners. These Candied Apples *are great as a side dish with duck, goose or pork.*

1 cup packed brown sugar
2 tablespoons butter
6 Granny Smith apples
Dash salt

❶ In large skillet, combine brown sugar and butter; heat until sugar is dissolved. Add apples and salt. Cook uncovered over very low heat about 1 hour, turning frequently until softened; serve.

8 servings

Preparation time: 15 minutes. Ready to serve: 1 hour 15 minutes.

Per serving: 190 calories, 3 g total fat (2 g saturated fat), 8 mg cholesterol, 65 mg sodium, 3 g fiber.

ROOT BEER CRANBERRIES OR MOUSSE

If you are not a root beer fan, use ginger ale or orange soda in this recipe.

1 (12-oz.) can or bottle root beer
1 (12-oz.) bag cranberries
1½ cups sugar
1 tablespoon cornstarch
4 cups heavy cream

❶ In large pot, bring root beer and cranberries to a boil. In small bowl, combine sugar and cornstarch; mix well. Add to root beer mixture; simmer 5 minutes or until liquid becomes clear and shiny. Chill cranberry mixture and serve.

❷ For 4 servings of mousse, beat cream at medium speed in large bowl until foamy and thick. Fold in 1 cup root beer mixture. In 4 tall, stemmed glasses, layer cream with root beer mixture to desired fullness. Refrigerate leftovers.

4 servings.

Preparation time: 5 minutes. Ready to serve: 20 minutes.

Per serving: 1075 calories, 75 g total fat (45 g saturated fat), 265 mg cholesterol, 100 mg sodium, 4 g fiber.

> **CHEF'S NOTES:**
>
> • Calvados or Grand Marnier may be added at the end. Add an additional 5 minutes cooking time to burn off alcohol.

ROAST PRIME RIB

There are a lot of wives' tales about cooking prime rib. In my opinion, this is the best way there is.

1	(4- to 6-lb.) prime rib or beef roast, bone-in
3	cups sliced onions (1/4 inch)
1/2	cup carrots chopped (1/2 inch)
1/2	cup celery chopped (1/2 inch)
2	garlic cloves
1	cup red wine
2	cups water

❶ Heat oven to 200°F.

❷ Place roaster rack in pan. Place roast fat side up on rack. Top with even layer of onions. Place uncovered in oven. Bake 3 hours or until internal temperature reaches 170°F; remove from oven.

❸ Place roast in shallow pan; remove onions. Cover roast with aluminum foil topped with clean kitchen towel; do not seal sides. Let rest 15 to 20 minutes.

❹ While meat is resting, increase oven temperature to 375°F. Remove rack from pan. Return onions to pan. Add carrots, celery and garlic; bake 15 minutes. With wooden spoon, stir vegetables and remove all drippings from bottom of pan. Transfer vegetables and liquid to large pot; add red wine and water. Bring to a slow rolling boil 4 minutes. Strain liquid into sauce bowl to serve with roast slices.

9 servings.

Preparation time: 5 minutes.
Ready to serve: 5 hours.

Per serving: 865 calories, 66 g total fat (27 g saturated fat), 215 mg cholesterol, 165 mg sodium, 0 g fiber.

CHEF'S NOTES:

• You can prepare prime rib roast (bone-in or boneless) this way.

• Do not salt and pepper roast. The salt draws out the juices and the pepper flavor does not permeate the fat cover. Let each diner season to taste.

• Do *not* start your oven at 375°F as this will cause the roast to lose moisture and flavor.

• This method of baking will create an evenly roasted, moist, flavorful roast.

• For extra flavor in the *au jus*, add 1 tablespoon beef base to the water before adding to saucepan. Do not use beef consommé, as it has its own flavor.

FOOD SAFTEY COOKING TEMPERATURES (°F)

	Medium	Well Done
Beef	160°	170°
Pork	160°	170°
Lamb	160°	170°
Veal	160°	170°
Veal, beef, lamb, pork (ground)		160°
Turkey (whole)		180°
Chicken (whole)		180°
Poultry (breasts, roasts)		170°
Poultry (thighs, wings)		180°
Turkey, Chicken (ground)		165°
Duck		180°
Goose		180°
Stuffing (cooked separately)		165°

This index lists every recipe in Today's Country Cooking *by name. If you're looking for a specific recipe but can't recall the exact name, turn to the General Index that starts on page 166.*

GENERAL INDEX

There are several ways to use this helpful index. First — you can find recipes by name. If you don't know a recipe's specific name but recall a main ingredient or the cooking technique, look under that heading and all the related recipes will be listed; scan for the recipe you want. If you have an ingredient or cooking technique in mind and want to find a great recipe for it, look under that heading as well to find a list of recipes to choose from. Finally — you can use this general index to find a summary of the recipes in each chapter of the book (basic recipes, lunch, supper, etc.).

RECIPES AND NOTES

RECIPES AND NOTES

RECIPES AND NOTES

RECIPES AND NOTES

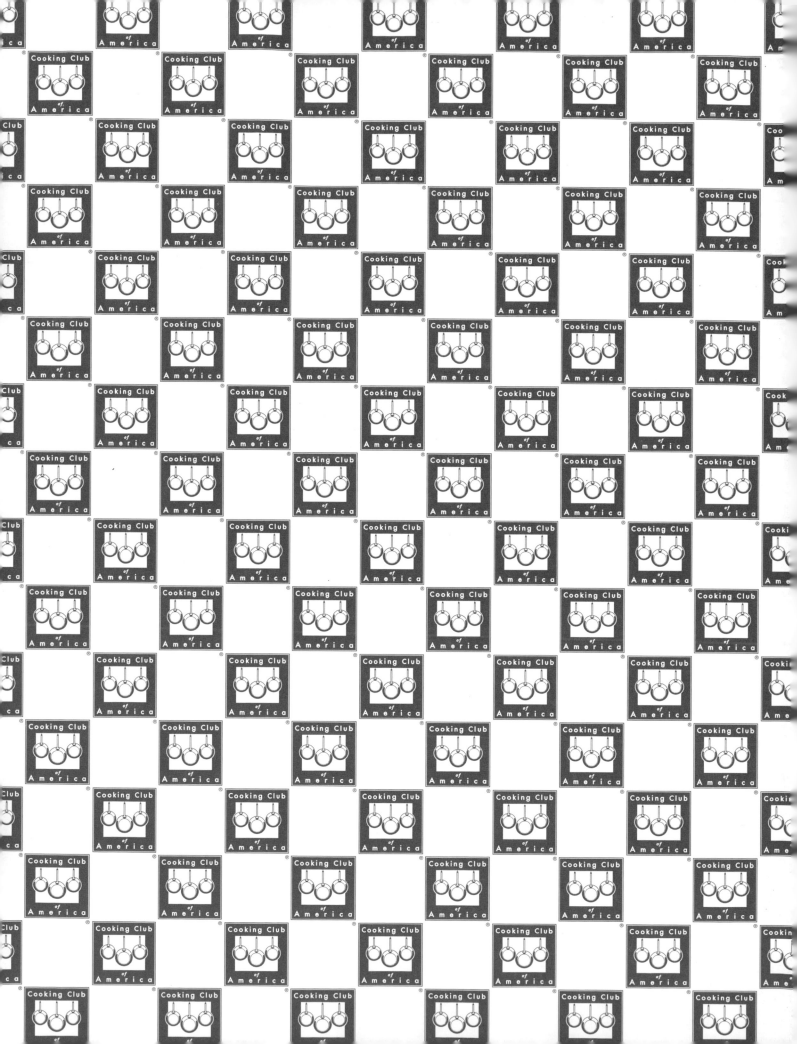